The Bully, The Bullied and Beyond

Help for Bullies, Victims and Bystanders
Grades 5-12

By Esther Williams, M.Ed., L.P.C.

© 2007, 2005 by YouthLight, Inc.
Chapin, SC 29036

Design and Layout by Diane Florence • Project Editing by Susan Bowman

ISBN
1-889636-76-2

Library of Congress Number
2005925312

10 9 8 7 6 5 4 3
Printed in the United States

youth light
inc.

PO Box 115 • Chapin, SC 29036

(800) 209-9774 • (803) 345-1070 • Fax (803) 345-0888

yl@youthlightbooks.com • www.youthlightbooks.com

The Bully, The Bullied and Beyond
Strategies for Schools, Teachers and Parents
Help for Bullies, Victims and Bystanders
For grades 5 - 12

TABLE OF CONTENTS

THE BULLY, THE BULLIED AND BEYOND

Introduction

Unit One
Bullying in School: School-Wide Strategies

Unit Two
Bullying in the Classroom – Skills for Teachers

Unit Three
Families Make a Difference – Skills for Parents

Unit Four
Empowering the Bystander – Skills for Students

Unit Five
Learning a Better Way – Skills for Bullies

Unit Six
Helping the Victim – Skills for the Bullied

Unit Seven
Helping the Victim with Special Needs – Skills for Students With Disabilities

ABOUT THE AUTHOR:

Esther Williams was a middle school teacher and a school counselor at the middle school, elementary school and alternative school levels. She has twenty-five years experience in public education. Esther was a middle school counselor during the 1990's when victims of bullying began to use guns and violence to call attention to their pain. This spurred her to research bullying and to provide intervention that would make sure the students in her school were safe and bullying was effectively addressed. She is a Licensed Professional Counselor in private practice in Auburn AL. She consults with schools systems throughout the United States on numerous school related issues including bullying, anger management, ADHD and student motivation. Her first book, Breaking Down the Wall of Anger, is an anger management curriculum and is available through YouthLight, Inc.

Esther is available to provide training for this book as well as many other educational topics. If you would like to contact her to comment on this book or to receive a listing of her workshops, please E-Mail her at esther@positivepaths.com.

DEDICATION

As I completed this book and began to feel a pride in writing a book on bullying, a long overdue shame flooded my consciousness. How could I present myself as an "expert" on stopping bullying when I myself was a bully when I was in school? I was part of a group of girls (I say that not as an excuse but because that is how female bullying usually works) who used social isolation to bully another girl. After many phone calls, leaving messages and finally writing a letter, I was able to find Sherrill, the girl who was bullied, and we agreed to have lunch. I made a long overdue apology for my behavior and asked for her forgiveness. I will forever appreciate her willingness to forgive.

I told Sherrill about my book and asked her if I could dedicate the book to her. I can not go back and undo what the other girls and I did to her but my hope is that through this book others will not have to know the pain that Sherrill went through or the delayed shame that I felt. I dedicate this book to Sherrill Nixon and all the other victims of bullying. I hope it will be some comfort to them that people are beginning to take their pain seriously.

ACKNOWLEDGEMENTS:

It is not often that you have a friend who will read a document of this length and give you constructive suggestions. I am so grateful to my good friend Linda Silavant who made this book better through her suggestions. I value her friendship and opinion more that she realizes.

People say that the satisfaction of having a book published is like giving birth to a child. But in my life, nothing compares to the joy of watching my two children become interesting adults. Thank you both for enriching my life and showering me with blessings. I am very proud of Elizabeth and Harrison.

My greatest supporter in life is my husband of 33 years, Perry. He inspires and helps me in ways that he can't imagine.

As always, thank you God.

The Bully, The Bullied and Beyond

Help for Bullies, Victims and Bystanders
Grades 5-12

INTRODUCTION

EVERYBODY LOVES RAYMOND
A Story of Inspiration

Raymond was a thirty-two year old man who came to my counseling office to work on anger related issues. It didn't take long for the pain of his childhood to start pouring out. Raymond had an abusive father. His father had one of those "Jekyll and Hyde" personalities. At times he appeared to be the perfect caring father and in an instant he could become cruel, abusive and violent. Raymond never knew how his father was going to come home on any given day.

As Raymond was telling his story he began telling stories of abuse and bullying at school. Raymond described horrible bullying on the school bus. Older students who sat at the back of the bus abused and bullied Raymond. He said "Every day I was their source of entertainment." The bus driver knew what was happening but did nothing (If you start an anti-bullying program, be sure to include bus drivers.) He could not tell his abusive father about what was happening on the bus and he never told anyone in the school. As Raymond told these long past stories of bullying, the pain on his face was as raw as if it had happened yesterday.

When Raymond was in the 7th grade, his father lost his job. Here is an abusive family and now we add extreme economic stresses. This was the year that Raymond grew about three inches. Because there was no money, Raymond had to continue wearing clothes that were too little for him. He said "Every kid at the school made fun of my clothes." Raymond went to a middle school that leveled their students on ability. Raymond was in section "C." It was not hard to figure out that section "A's" was the top group and he wasn't in it. Raymond told me "No one thought I was very smart, I had never made all "A's," and we all know that making all "A's" is what means you are smart. As he told these stories I could just see the tall skinny kid sitting in the back of the "section C class" in clothes too little, just wanting to disappear and not be noticed. His future doesn't look too bright does it?

Raymond had a 7th grade teacher, Juanita Patrick. Ms. Patrick gave Raymond a gift that changed this life; in fact it may have saved his life. She encouraged Raymond. He told me, with a puzzled look on his face, "She told me I was smart. I don't know why she said that? She told me that I could learn this." Raymond continued, "I knew I had to work harder than the other kids, but I did because Ms. Patrick told me I was smart." Because Raymond worked harder he began making "A's." At the end of that year, Mrs. Patrick went to the principal and insisted that Raymond be put in section "A" for the next school year. Having someone express that much confidence in him gave Raymond a tremendous boost of self-assurance and reinforced his belief that he was as smart as the other kids. In the 8th grade, he was in section "A" and for the first time in his whole life he made all "A's" all year.

Raymond only made one "B" while in high school. He graduated from Auburn University with a degree in history. Raymond went to the University of Alabama Law School. He finished third in his law school class. Raymond sat in my office as a successful lawyer and said with every assurance in his voice, "I never would have become a lawyer, if it hadn't been for Ms. Patrick." One teacher, one year changed his life because she chose to encourage a tall skinny kid with clothes that were too little. Although she was not able to stop the abuse at home or on the bus, because she never knew about it, she gave him hope and confidence through words of encouragement.

There are many "Raymonds" in your school and in your classrooms today. All they need is one caring adult. Find Raymond, change his life, be his Ms. Patrick.

WHY DEAL WITH BULLYING?

Bullying is a problem in every school in the United States and schools throughout the world. Every day, in every school, there are students who are having their quality of life depreciated by cruel, malicious incidents of bullying. Whether the student is being bullied, bullying others, or witnessing bullying behaviors, he/she is being diminished by the experience. Bullying generally begins in the elementary grades, peaks in the sixth through eighth grades, and persists into high school according to a 2001 report from the *Office of Juvenile Justice and Delinquency Prevention.*

There is nothing new about bullying. Unfortunately, bullying has been going on as long as there have been schools. But the pervasiveness of bullying doesn't mean that schools should accept it as inevitable. Bullying has received a lot of attention in recent years. Students who were being teased and picked on began to respond to their abuse by bringing guns to school. A study funded by the

U.S. Secret Service found that two-thirds of the 41 youths involved in deadly school shootings since 1974 said they had been seriously bullied at school and that revenge was one of their motives. The shootings at Columbine high school in 1999 was the event that made educators finally consider the possibility that ignoring bullying could be dangerous. Unfortunately, some educators still fail to take the problem of bullying seriously.

Bullying is the most frequently occurring form of violence in schools. Former Attorney General Janet Reno stated:

"Youth violence has been one of the greatest single crime problems we face in this country. Youth who commit crimes of violence must be held accountable, and the punishment must be firm and fair and fit the crime. At the same time, we must do everything we can to prevent crime in the first place. It is critical that we do all we can to identify young people who need our help, and then get them the help they need."

We must ask ourselves if our very culture promotes bullying. We live in a society where wealth and power are valued and admired. Movie heroes often use bullying and violence to "settle the score." John Wayne and Sylvester Stallone never went to conflict-resolution classes. Is it surprising then, that students have learned to imitate their heroes? We live in a society where the tough guy is valued and the weak and frail are often pitied and even despised. Reports indicate that bullies tend to be more respected and admired among their peers and many consider bullying behaviors normal. Many students know that if you are a friend of the bully, you are less likely to become his/her victim.

Violence isn't the only form of bullying promoted by the media. Students watch game shows where the host insults the contestants – "You are the weakest link" and contestants are also encouraged to insult their competitors. The message the entertainment industry often sends viewers is that insulting people is funny. Most people spend more time discussing the insults that the American Idol judge, Simon, makes to contestants than they do the performances of the contestants themselves. When schools address bullying, it can mean confronting some deeply ingrained cultural attitudes.

As educators, we must do more than pass on facts and information. We must help all students develop skills that will serve them well throughout their lives. We must provide them with opportunities to learn skills that will help them not only survive, but thrive in a culture that values strength and power. We want to send out into our communities students who respect authority, themselves and others. We want students who can communicate their needs in non-violent ways and can show respect for the needs of others. We must help our students develop the ability to stand up for their rights while respecting the rights of others. These skills are not measured on any of our standardized tests, but we as educators know that these skills are far more critical to our students' future well-being than much of the information we are drilling into their heads each day. Bullying is a learned behavior, and it can be unlearned. There are no simple solutions or easy answers, but it is critical that we try.

WHAT IS BULLYING?

Bullying is a conscious, willful, repeated and deliberately hostile act intended to inflict pain, discomfort, embarrassment, and/or induce fear through violence, the threat of violence or humiliation. Bullying can be any gesture, written or verbal expression, or physical act that a reasonable person should know will hurt another person, damage another student's property, place another student in reasonable fear of harm to the student's person, or damage to the student's property. In bullying situations, there is always an imbalance of power between the bully and the victim. The bully consciously abuses their power and demonstrates a consistent pattern of disrespect for their victim.

Bullying can be perpetrated either by an individual or a group. It can be "in your face" or behind your back and can take many forms including:

- **Verbal abuse** – teasing, name-calling, mocking, taunting and putdowns.

- **Emotional cruelty** – isolation, rejection, ignoring, spreading rumors and manipulating others.

- **Physical violence** – hitting, kicking, pushing, slapping, spitting, tripping, choking, the taking of or defacing property and physical acts that demean and humiliate.

- **Harassment** – threats, extortion, coercion and ethnic, racial, religious and sexual taunting.

- **Electronic persecution** – bullying behaviors via the Internet or cell phone.

Bullies may use prejudice related to race, gender, religion, physical attributes, or mental abilities to justify their behavior or they often make their attack without any real motive, other than that they see their victim as an easy target. Bullying disrupts and interferes with the school's educational mission.

SEXUAL HARASSMENT

Harassment is a kind of bullying in which the victim is repeatedly treated badly by a stronger person or group because of his/her membership in a group (racial, religious, ethnic, gender, or sexual orientation).

Sexual harassment means that someone is treated differently because of his or her sex. The sexual harassment of students is taking place daily on every school campus in America. **Sexual harassment is against the law, and schools must protect their students from it.**

A 7-year-old girl in Minnesota complained of being harassed daily on her school bus by a group of boys. The boys requested oral sex and made comments about her body. The girl's mother notified the school authorities. Two students were removed from the bus and school officials talked to the students. The school district was forced to pay damages for not acting more strongly on the young girl's behalf.

The American Association of University Women surveyed 1,632 students between the 8th and 11th grades. They found that girls are much more upset by sexual harassment than are boys. Too many people still believe that girls secretly like sexual attention and those girls "ask for it" by the way they walk or dress. The A.A.U.W. survey reported that:

- 85% of girls and 76% of boys reported being sexually harassed at some point in school;

- 20% were victimized by an adult and 80% by another student;

- 64% of the girls and 21% of the boys reported feeling highly embarrassed by the sexual harassment;

- 43% of the girls and 8% of the boys felt less confident after the harassment;

- 39% of the girls and 8% of the boys said they were fearful as a result of the abuse;

- 30 to 50% of all child molesters are juveniles and 90% of juvenile sexual offenders are male;

- 87% of the girls and 85% of the boys indicated that they would be very upset if they were called gay or lesbian.

The Gay, Lesbian and Straight Education Network released the 2003 National School Climate Survey results.

- 84% of gay students report being verbally, sexually or physically harassed at school;

- 83% of gay students report that faculty never or rarely intervened;

- Students who are gay reported significant levels of verbal harassment;

- Gay students are twice as likely to report they do not intend to go to college and their GPA's are significantly lower (2.9 versus 3.3);

- 40% of gay students are likely to skip school because they are too afraid to go.

WHAT CAN SCHOOLS DO ABOUT SEXUAL HARASSMENT?

Help students understand that sexual harassment is inappropriate; it is hurtful and disrespectful of the victim. Sexual harassment is behavior or words that:

- Are uninvited, unwanted and unwelcome;
- Cause a person to feel uncomfortable or offended;
- Create an environment that makes learning difficult;

Explain to students that sexual harassment can take many forms:

Physical
- Standing in someone's way or standing too close;
- Bumping into someone or brushing against the person on purpose;
- Patting, hugging, grabbing, touching or pinching.

Verbal
- Comments about a person's body;
- Sexual jokes, stories remarks or rumors;
- Notes, letters or graffiti;
- Whistles or rude noises.

Nonverbal
- Staring at someone's body;
- Showing sexual pictures or drawings;
- Gestures such as licking lips or suggestive body movements.

Establish school policies against sexual harassment.
Identify specific, progressive consequences for harassers.
Encourage students to report incidents of sexual harassment.

ELECTRONIC BULLYING

Bullying has moved beyond "slam books" and name-calling to high-tech electronic attacks. Students can no longer feel safe from bullying in their homes. *The University of New Hampshire's Crimes Against Children Research Center* conducted a study on Internet bullying in 2000. Researchers found that one in 17 children ages 10 to 17 had been threatened or harassed online and that about one-third of those found the incidents extremely distressing. The rumors, threats, and humiliation are nothing new, but the Internet allows a new vehicle for bullies to pass their message of hate to thousands of people with the click of a key. Websites and screen names give bullies a cloak of anonymity, making them difficult to trace. Cyber-bullies can spread rumors, threaten others, and generally make life miserable for their victims throughout the day and night. Cyber-bullies are typically middle-class students who are usually thought of as "good kids." The Internet allows bullies to say things that they would never say face to face, and it gives them a sense of security and power.

The Internet and text messaging makes students vulnerable to bullying in new ways. The most common form of electronic bullying is instant messaging, or "IM's". Bullies can send a mean or threatening "IM's" with no identification beyond a selected screen-name. If that name gets blocked, they simply choose another one. Bullies have used Websites to vote on the ugliest or fattest student in school, or create a Website devoted to smearing one individual. Electronic bullies have also used photo-editing tools to paste a student's face onto a pornographic or unflattering photo, and then disseminate the photo to thousands of students. The possibilities of online bullying are only beginning to become fully explored.

More recently, cell phones are being used to bully via text-messaging and cell-phone photos. An overweight student in Japan had cell-phone pictures secretly taken of him while he was changing in the locker room. The pictures were then sent via the Internet to many of his peers (*Christian Science Monitor*, Dec. 30 2003.)

The most infamous online incident to date involved a Canadian teenager who has become known as "the Star Wars kid." The young man filmed himself acting out a scene from the movie "Star Wars." Some of his peers got the video and uploaded it to the Internet. Special effects and sounds were added. The boy is now the most downloaded male of 2003. According to news reports, this young man has dropped out of school and is now receiving psychiatric help (*Christian Science Monitor*, Dec. 30, 2003).

WHAT CAN SCHOOLS DO ABOUT ELECTRONIC BULLYING?

Schools can feel helpless when dealing with online bullying. Cyberspace is a vast new territory, and schools aren't sure how far to extend their jurisdiction. Free-speech rights can make it difficult to take down a Website, and bullies are often anonymous. Even though most of the harassment takes place off school property, the effects can carry over into the school. Schools must understand the correlation between electronic bullying at home and a safe environment at school. Despite the difficulties, parents, students, and schools need to address cyber-bullying.

The most effective techniques to fight cyber-bullying are the same ones that fight bullying of any kind:

- Students should be encouraged to report incidents of online bullying and not protect the perpetrator;

- Students should be instructed not to participate in spreading mean "IMs" and refuse to go to websites designed to hurt others;

- Teachers need to discuss electronic bullying with their students and encourage them to sign a pledge to ethically use the Internet, e-mail and phone;

- The school should include online bullying in the school's anti-bullying policy and identify it as an offense that can be punished by school officials;

- Policies concerning Internet and cell-phone use should be sent home at the beginning of the school year. Some schools have chosen to ban cell phones altogether;

- Schools need to provide information to all parents concerning electronic bullying and encourage them to monitor their child's Internet and phone usage;

- Parents should be informed when the school becomes aware of specific problems resulting from online bullying;

- Students being harassed by cyber-bullies need to make a note of the time and date of each message received. They should alert their Internet or wireless service provider to the problem, and the provider may be willing to change their e-mail address or cell-phone number for free. If the offending messages do not stop, victims may want to go to the police.

RESEARCH ON BULLYING

In 2003, the National Institute of *Child Health and Human Development* surveyed 15,686 students in grades 6-10 in public and private schools throughout the United States. The survey found:

- 17 % had been bullied weekly;

- 19 % had bullied others weekly;

- 6 % had both bullied others and been bullied themselves;

- The frequency of bullying was similar among whites, blacks and Hispanics, and children in cities, towns, suburbs, and rural areas were equally likely to be victims;

- Both bullies and victims were more likely than other students to report psychological and social problems;

- Bullies exhibited higher rates of alcohol and tobacco use and tended to express more negative attitudes toward school;

- Victims were more likely to report feelings of loneliness and difficulty making friends;

- Victims suffered humiliation, insecurity, and loss of self-esteem and were at greater risk of suffering from depression and other mental health problems;

- Boys were more likely to be involved in bullying and violent behaviors than were girls;

- About 6 % of students reported that they were both victims and bullies; and these students are believed to be at the highest risk.

RESEARCH ON STUDENT VIOLENCE

The *National Institute of Child Health and Human Development* (NICHHD) survey in 2003 found a significant correlation between bullying and violence:

- Both students who bullied and their victims were more likely to engage in violent behaviors themselves;

- Students who bully were at the greatest risk for violence;

- Of boys who said they had bullied others, 52% reported carrying a weapon in the past month, 43% had carried a weapon to school, 38% were involved in frequent fights, and 46% reported having been injured in a fight;

- Of boys who said they had been bullied in school, 36% had carried a weapon, 29% had taken a weapon to school, 23% were involved in frequent fights, and 32% said they had been injured in a fight;

- Boys who bullied others when they were away from school were at the greatest risk of engaging in violence behaviors;

- Of boys who had bullied others while away from school, 70% had carried a weapon, 58% had carried a weapon in school, 45% said they fought frequently, and 56% percent had been injured in a fight.

HOW TO USE THIS BOOK

This book is designed to be used by **administrators, guidance counselors, teachers** and other **school personnel** who work with students. The unit titles state their intended use. The student activities are numerically identified. The first number identifies the unit and the second number identifies the activity. (Ex: Activity 4.7 is the seventh activity in Unit Four.) Most of the activities are suggested for use in the other units as well as the unit they are in. Many of the skills taught in each of the units are applicable for most students in the school.

The **Introduction** contains research and information that can be valuable in educating everyone in the school community about bullying and the need for a comprehensive anti-bullying program.

Unit One provides helpful guidelines and suggestions for developing and implementing a school wide anti-bullying program and creating a positive school climate. **Administrators** and **leadership staff** who are concerned about the problem of bullying and want to develop school-wide programs need to use this unit as a guide for their program. This unit contains useful information, statistics, strategies, policies and surveys that can foster the development and implementation of comprehensive bullying prevention programs in a school setting. Comprehensive *bullying surveys* for the students, teachers and parents are found in this unit.

Unit Two contains information that can be especially helpful to the classroom **teacher** in creating a caring, bully-free classroom. Teachers will become more aware of bullying and the impact their behavior and classroom management style has on their students, and how to positively influence their students' behavior. This unit includes fun *student activities* that teachers or **counselors** can use in the classroom setting. The *student pledges* are included in this unit.

Unit Three includes helpful information on families and how to gain the support of **parents** when conducting an anti-bullying program in your school. There is helpful information that **teachers** and **administrators** can pass directly to parents to make them aware of the schools policies and how parents can effectively address the problem of bullying in their home.

Unit Four provides **teachers** and **counselors** with lots of great activities to use with *all students*. These activities are for *educating* students about bullying, *empowering* all students to respond to bullying, training in *confliction resolution* and appreciating *diversity*. All these activities are appropriate for large group instruction and many are also recommended in other units for use with small groups.

Unit Five contains lots of great *activities* to use with students who are exhibiting bullying behavior. **Counselors** and **teachers** can use these activities with *small groups* or *individuals* who need to *examine their behavior* and *learn skills* such as *relaxation, empathy, rational thoughts* and *learning to be kind*.

Unit Six includes many skill-building *activities* to use with students who are bullied. These easy to use activities can be utilized in *small groups* or with *individuals* by **teachers** or **counselors**. These fun activities will help students learn skills such as *assertiveness, safety, relaxation, friendship*, and twelve different strategies for feeling powerful through *non-aggressive responses* to bullying comments.

Unit Seven provides **teachers** and **counselors** with much needed information on *students with disorders and disabilities*. The information can be used to *educate all students* concerning disabilities that are often manifested in poor social skills. Other students frequently misunderstand this lack of socially acceptable behaviors. Unit seven includes over 50 easy to use suggestions for teaching children specific *nonverbal communications skills*. Activities that teach skills in friendship, safety, conflict resolution, etc. found in the other units, are references for use with students with disabilities.

Unit One
Bullying in School: School-wide Strategies

BULLYING IN SCHOOLS: SCHOOL-WIDE STRATEGIES

To educate a person in mind and not in morals is to educate a menace to society.

— Theodore Roosevelt, U.S. President

Unit One
BULLYING IN SCHOOL

Can you imagine your school with no students bullying or picking on one another? A school where all students are treating one another with respect and where bystanders have the skills to deal with bullying effectively and intervene in appropriate ways? If you cannot visualize your school bully-free, then you are part of the problem!

For too long, educators have accepted bullying as a normal part of the school experience. They have thrown up their hands and exclaimed that "it is just going to happen; there is nothing we can do about it." "Kids will be kids, and this is just going to happen." "It is part of growing up." "It is no big deal." These statements are **WRONG! Bullying *is* a big deal**. Children can and should be expected to be kind and considerate to one another. It is **not** a normal part of growing up. Bullying is mean, cruel, disrespectful and, in some cases, illegal. As long as educators accept bullying as normal behavior, it will continue. Decide right now, as a school, that bullying will stop, that it will not be tolerated! We, the education community must change our attitude toward bullying behaviors. They can no longer be tolerated. Bullying must be taken seriously or we will continue to read horrifying headlines of victims who chose to retaliate against their tormentors with violence and death.

School officials often feel overwhelmed with all the pressure they face and at times choose to ignore the impact bullying has. It is the responsibility of the schools to protect students. Erika Harold, 2003 *Miss America* chose bullying as her platform. In a *USA Today* article, Harold shared that in the 9th grade she was the victim of pervasive, severe racial and sexual harassment. "I was incessantly called names such as whore and slut. Teachers and school officials did little to help me. When I told one school official about my classmates' discussions of buying a rifle to shoot me, he suggested that my problems would end if I would only "be more submissive like the other girls." Harold was forced to transfer to another high school but she reported that her self-esteem, dignity and sense of optimism were greatly diminished. Harold issued a national call for schools to take a proactive, comprehensive approach to eradicating bullying behaviors from our schools.

BULLYING AND VIOLENCE

There is no question that many, if not all the school shooters of the late 1990's were the victims of pervasive bullying. Students in Pearl Mississippi taunted 16-year-old Luke Woodham calling him a "chubby nerd." On October 2, 1998, Woodham stabbed his mother to death and shot nine of his classmates, killing two. "I killed because people like me are mistreated every day," he explained in a letter (*Newsweek*, April 6, 1998). "My whole life I felt outcast, alone." Woodham, like many of the other school shooters in the 90's were victims not bullies. They felt powerless to stop the torments heaped on them by their peers until they got a gun in their hands. Then they felt very powerful. The *Bureau of Justice Statistics on School Crime and Safety*, reported that 2 out of 3 students reported that they know how to make a bomb, or know where to get the information to do it. As educators, we must protect the victim and help them feel powerful without resorting to violence.

Let's assume, for our own sanity if nothing else, that there will be no shootings at your school. Deadly violence, resulting from bullying is not an option at your school. Now, don't you feel better? Just because your school does not need metal detectors or police guards, it does not mean that students are physically and emotionally safe there. Every day, students at your school are being laughed at, taunted, intimidated and abused. In a thousand different ways they are being stripped of their dignity and their very soul wounded. Every day, students are leaving your school with emotional wounds that will leave them scarred for the rest of their lives. Students can be in a great deal of pain with no visible wounds. Educators must get serious about protecting them.

BULLYING AND LEARNING

If you are still not convinced that bullying is a problem on your campus, consider the following: students can not learn, work or thrive in an environment where they do not feel safe. Psychologist Abraham Maslow identifies what he calls the "Hierarchy of Needs." Maslow maintains that until the primary needs in his hierarchy are met, the other needs do not matter. Maslow proposes that as humans, our most basic needs are those of oxygen, food, clothing and shelter. Certainly if we do not have access to oxygen, nothing else matters. Following this reasoning, if students are hungry, they are less interested in other activities, such as learning. This is one reason public schools provide breakfast and lunch programs.

Second on Maslow's "Hierarchy of Needs" is safety. If students do not feel safe (both emotionally and physically) things like learning just don't matter. The *National Education Association* estimates that 160,000 children miss school every day due to fear of attack or intimidation by other students. In fact the report indicated that probably 15% of all school absenteeism is directly related to fears of being bullied at school. The 2003 report of the *Gay, Lesbian and Straight Education Network* states that as many as 40% of gay students are likely to skip school because they are too afraid to go. Students certainly can not learn if they are not at school. The National Association of Secondary School Principals surveyed 65,000 sixth through twelfth-graders in 1993. At that time, 37% reported that they did not feel safe in school, and 63 % felt they would learn more if they could feel safer and wanted classes in anger management and conflict resolution. I would imagine these statistics would be much higher today. *USA Today* reported that a national poll of 11 to 17 year-olds found that 71% worried they might get shot or stabbed at school. The students fear seems very justified when we read the *Bureau of Justice* statistics which reported that 282,000 students are physically attacked in secondary schools each month.

When students are constantly concerned about their safety, they are less likely to move through Maslow's "Hierarchy of Needs" to self-actualization. When you address bullying in your school, students will feel safer, learning will be enhanced and students will be better able to develop into emotionally healthy adults. Or another way of putting it that will get your attention: if students feel safe they are more likely to come to school, they can better concentrate on learning and TEST SCORES will improve! School time devoted to learning to get along, dealing with anger and conflicts in non-violent ways can pay off in a multitude of ways.

ANTI-BULLYING PROGRAMS MAKE A DIFFERENCE

Anti-bullying programs are effective and bullying can be reduced. It is embarrassing how far behind the United States is in addressing the problem of bullying. In 1982, three boys in Norway, all victims of severe bullying at school, committed suicide within a few months of each other in different parts of the country. Following these incidents, **Dan Olweus**, a professor of psychology at the **University of Bergen in Norway**, surveyed 150,000 students to develop a comprehensive program to address bullying in Norway. Olweus's approach achieved a fifty percent reduction in bullying in the two years following the campaign. In addition, antisocial behavior in general, such as theft, vandalism, and truancy showed a marked drop and students reported more satisfaction with school (*Education Digest*, March 1988).

At McCormick Middle School in McCormick County, S.C., a survey revealed that nearly half of the students had been bullied. The school launched an anti-bullying campaign including prevention programs, rules concerning bullying, clear punishments for bullying and a strong parent component. One year into the program, the number of students who reported they had been bullied dropped from nearly half to 22 percent (*Education Week*, August/September 1997).

In 1992, McNair Elementary in Hazelwood, MO, began a comprehensive program to teach students to respond appropriately when they felt they were being bullied. The year before the program went into effect: McNair reported fifty-five fights and the year after the program only 6. An additional bonus was that the school's standardized math and reading scores rose from the 40th to the 60th percentile. Laurel Elementary in Fort Collins, CO, indicated that behavior infractions fell 66% after implementing various initiatives regarding bullying. (*Time*, Let Bullies Beware, April 2, 2001)

Anti-bullying programs must be more that just hanging posters around the school or holding an assembly. To be effective the program must be sustained over time, and that is often hard for most schools to do. Experts say the key to stopping bullying is to teach tolerance and to establish a school climate in which parents are involved and students feel comfortable reporting incidents.

ZERO TOLERANCE: DOES IT WORK?

Some schools are cracking down on bullying with harsh zero-tolerance policies that are more puni-tive than educational. These policies often do not give administrators any discretion when dealing with a student offense. The *National Center on Education Statistics* report that eighty percent of schools employ some form of zero tolerance. Zero tolerance rules that are automatic and unyield-ing can lead to suspensions and alternative school placement for students who are little or no risk to other students. In 2002, a 16 year-old honor student in Texas was expelled for one year when a non-serrated bread knife was found in the bed of his pickup. It is believed that the knife had fallen out of a box he had taken to Goodwill. In 2000, an 11-year-old in Georgia was suspended for 10 days because she took her "Tweety Bird" wallet with a small 10-inch chain to class. School officials said the chain could be a weapon and violated their zero tolerance policy. Almost daily stories are reported of school authorities overreacting to harmless or unintentional offenses. What has happened to using good judgment?

Some students are even being punished for their thoughts under zero tolerance policies. A 4th-grad-er in Florida received a 10-day suspension for drawing a picture of him shooting another student with a laser gun. The suspended student told school authorities he drew the picture because the child represented in the picture had been teasing him and calling him names. Drawing the picture was certainly an expression of a need to be protected from teasing. Does anyone think this 9 year-old child actually intended to carry out this act? How does a 10-day suspension for the victim of teasing, who was "expressing a threat," make anyone at this elementary school safer? In Los Angeles, a 12th-grade student was expelled for creating a "dangerous atmosphere" after complaining to the principal in a letter about the lack of free speech within the school. The student ended his letter with, "In this wonderful country in which I am allowed to fully express myself… SILENCE=DEATH! School authorities must begin addressing the problem instead of trying to suppress the behavior.

While zero tolerance policies may be well intentioned, there is evidence that they not only don't reduce misconduct but they also may produce other negative consequences. More that 3 million students were suspended in the 2000-2001 school year, according to the *U.S. Department of Education*. Schools with high rates of suspension, also report high rates of school-dropouts and increases in juvenile-crime rates, reports *Harvard University's Civil Rights Project*. Russell Skiba of *Indiana University's Safe and Responsive Schools Project* examined the effectiveness of zero tolerance in a 2000 study. Skiba found that schools with such policies are no more orderly or secure than schools that evaluate behavior problems case by case.

Many schools are abandoning zero tolerance for a graduated discipline system that also provides counseling for troubled students to help them cope better with bullying and conflict. When Clearwater High School in Florida abandoned zero tolerance for a more a more balanced approach, their suspension rate dropped by sixty-five percent over four years. The school's dropout rate and frequency of classroom disruptions also decreased, and test scores improved (*USA Today*, 2003.) *The American Bar Association* passed a resolution in 2002 opposing zero tolerance policies in schools. The resolution proposes that school should respond to student misbehavior in a fair and individual-ized manner.

PLANNING A SCHOOL WIDE ANTI-BULLYING CAMPAIGN

A school-wide anti-bullying campaign that is broad-based and involves all students and staff will be the most effective and have the greatest impact. Parents, teachers, students, administrators, and hopefully business and community leaders should be encouraged to participate in the planning and implementation of a multifaceted program. While all participants are important to the success of the program, the **principal** is the most important person to have involved in the campaign. Without strong support from the principal and the entire administrative team, the success of your efforts will be limited. The principal must provide active moral leadership before the students, parents and staff will take the program seriously. You will need to involve **students** in all aspects of the program. The more student involvement you have, the more effective your program will be.

I. Evaluate the problem.

- One of the mistakes we as educators often make is trying to solve a problem before we have evaluated the problem. The first step in addressing bullying is to identify the type and extent of the problem; then we can identify strategies to address bullying on the campus. (Unit One - *Evaluate the Problem, Collecting Data On Bullying, Activities 2.1 What Is Bullying? & 2.2 Style of Bullying.*)

II. Begin with education.

- Educate all staff members on the problem of bullying and its long-term consequences. The best way to gain the support of the staff is to educate them on the problem of bullying. This is best done by allocating a half-day or even a full day for the training session. Whether you bring in an outside "expert" or use current staff members, an effort should be made to gain consensus from all staff to support the anti-bullying program. The material from the Introduction, Unit One – *Bullying in School, Bullying and Violence, Bullying and Learning, Anti-Bullying Programs Make a Difference, Zero Tolerance – Does It Work?* & Unit Two - *Skills for Teachers* can be used to help educate staff members. **All staff** members need to be in agreement that bullying is always inappropriate. Information from the surveys should to be shared with the staff and an effort should be made to gain their input on how to address problem areas that have been identified. Certain staff will need to receive training on how to use the Activities in Unit Four - *Skills for Students*, Unit Five – *Skills for Bullies*, Unit Six - *Skills for the Bullied* and Unit Seven – *Skills for Students With Disabilities* sections of this book with students.

- Offer **parent and community members** training through classroom or assembly programs. Use material from the Introduction and Unit Three - *Skills for Parents* sections of this book to develop training for parents and/or provide some of the material to your parents. Be sure to involve parents in the planning of your anti-bullying program and encourage them to participate in activities. An effort should be made to open the lines of communication with parents on the issue of bullying. Encourage parents to work within the school program to address the problem concerning their children. Make a commitment to improve communication with the families of the victims and bullies, and provide education and support.

- Provide classroom instruction for **all students** about bullying and its consequences. Instruct teachers to hold discussions on the issue of bullying in their classrooms. Use activities from this book with all students. (Unit Four - *Skills for Students*)

III. Plan high-profile activities for the school.

- Invite speakers to address the student body or classrooms promoting pro-social or anti-bullying issues.
- Have clubs sponsor activities such as "No More Bullying" Day (Week or Month). The office can keep a record of reports of bullying and report progress to the student body.
- Support a "Unity Day" where students wear their school colors or wear white ribbons to symbolize peace.
- Promote a "Smile Day," where students are each given a smile card and hand the card to the first person to smile at them.
- Conduct a "Kindness Campaign" where students are encouraged to perform acts of kindness. Students can be recognized for their act of kindness.
- Post the number of days gone by without a fight on a display board or the school marquee.
- Sponsor a contest to generate an anti-bullying slogan for the school.
- Have students make posters promoting an anti-bullying theme. Display them throughout the school.
- Encourage students to sign no-bullying pledges. (Activity 2.3 Pledges)
- Locate a community sponsor to provide buttons or ribbons for students and staff to wear with anti-bullying slogans.
- Continue to keep anti-bullying themes going throughout the school year.

IV. Demonstrate the commitment of the school administration and staff to addressing the problem of bullying.

- Have highly visible administrative leadership that has a vision for the school and models respect by how he/she treats all students and staff.
- Expect all the staff to model positive, respectful and supportive behaviors. (Unit Two – *Skills for Teachers*)
- Insist that the faculty members demonstrate acceptance of individual differences and emphasize caring for others as much as they recognize good grades. (Unit One – *Promote Equity and Respect*)
- Provide additional supervision during unstructured times and in high-problem areas. (Unit One – *Physical Modifications and Increased Supervision*)
- Work to improve communication among school administrators, teachers, parents and students. (Unit One – *Anti-Bullying Policy*, Unit Seven – *Skills for Parents.*)
- Establish a referral system that is confidential and brings students who need help to the attention of the administration. (Unit One – *Reporting Bullying Behavior, Evaluating Reports of Bullying, Student Reporting Policy*)
- Develop policies for dealing with "at-risk" students and student threats. (Unit One – *School Response To Threats, Assessing a Threat, Assessing High Risk Factors For Students & School Dynamics*)
- Provide specialized training for both victims of bullying and the bullies themselves. (Unit Five – *Skills for Bullies*, Unit Six – *Skills for the Victim*, Unit Seven – *Skills for Students With Disabilities*)

V. Develop a school-wide discipline policy that upholds and promotes the school's values of respect for all students and prohibits bullying in any form.

- School policies should include proactive as well as reactive strategies for dealing with bullying and other discipline problems. (Unit One – *Developing Discipline Policies*, Unit Two – *The Teacher As The Model, Teacher Interventions For Bullies, Consequences For Angry Students*, Unit Five – *Skills for Bullies*)

- Consequences for violation of the discipline policy should be non-violent and consistently administered. (Unit Five – *Skills for Bullies Activities*)
- Students, parents and staff need to be involved in the development of discipline policies. (Unit One – *Developing Discipline Policies, Activity 2.8 Class Rules About Bullying*)
- The discipline policy should contain the rights of all students and the responsibilities of students who witness acts of misconduct. (Unit Four – *Skills for Students*)
- Students should be required to take responsibility for improving their behavior by signing behavioral contracts when appropriate and must be held accountable. (Unit Two – *Student Behavior Contracts*)
- The discipline plan should contain an anti-bullying policy, with a strong statement that bullying will not be tolerated. (Unit One – *Anti-Bullying Policy*)

VI. Integrate pro-social skills into the school curriculum.

- Offer classes in anger management, problem solving, self-esteem, and conflict resolution. Encourage all students to participate in these classes (Unit Two – *Teaching Caring Through The Curriculum*, Unit Five – *Skills for Students*).
- Implement programs such as peer tutoring and peer mediation (Unit Four – *Activity 4.16 Mediation Works*).
- Incorporate communication, friendship and assertiveness skills in all classrooms (Unit One – *Friendship Teams*, Unit Two – *Skills for Teachers*)
- Encourage all teachers to use cooperative learning in their classrooms.
- Teach character education as a vital part of the total curriculum. (Unit Four – *Skills for Students*)
- Instruct students and staff on the appreciation for and awareness of diversity. (Unit One – *Promote Equity and Respect, Activity 4.17 Strength From Diversity*)
- Provide students with a variety of opportunities for school, community-service, and service-learning projects. Encourage all students to participate in the service of others. (Unit One – *Mix It Up At Lunch, Friendship Teams, Opportunities for Community Service.*)

VII. Develop a school-wide sense of community and create a school climate in which all students believe they have worth, are capable human beings, are expected to serve and can resolve conflicts nonviolently.

- Offer extracurricular activities geared toward a variety of gifts, talents and interests. If students express an interest, create a club and assign a sponsor. (Art, drama, cooking, photography, computers, etc.)
- Provide opportunities for most students to participate in extracurricular activities by keeping participation cost low and being sensitive to transportation needs. Participation in extracurricular activities enhances students' sense of belonging and connection to other students, sponsors and the school.
- Require all students and staff to demonstrate a high level of good sportsmanship. Coaches have a wonderful opportunity to influence students in a positive way. Encourage the athletic staff to give their team and fans a sportsmanship score after each competition. Incidents of bullying by school athletes should be seriously addressed.
- Use school newsletters, assemblies and PA announcements to report good news stories, deliver inspirational quotes, encourage school unity and create a sense of community.

EVALUATING THE PROBLEM OF BULLYING

One mistake schools often make is they begin an Anti-Bullying program with out first evaluating and identifying specific problems. To determine what strategies you are going to include in your program, you need to know what type of bullying is going on, where it is occurring and how often. It is important to survey students, because research shows that most bullying takes place without teachers and administrators even being aware of it. Bullying incidents usually last less than fifteen seconds and over half are over within 34 seconds. Playground statistics indicate that every 7 minutes a student is bullied and only 4% of the time is there adult intervention. There is peer intervention 11% of the time and no intervention 85% of the time (Bureau of Justice Statistics.) Often times, teachers and administrators are not able to accurately describe the bullying problem on their campuses. Students need to know their input is needed and wanted and that it will be taken seriously.

Identify the "styles" of bullying.
Bullying can take many forms.

Verbal bullying is the most common form of bullying among both boys and girls. Verbal bullying can include teasing, name-calling, mocking, taunting, and putdowns. Although gestures and dirty looks are a form of non-verbal communication, they are going to be included as a form of verbal bullying.

Emotional bullying may be more subtle than the other forms but it is just as, if not more, painful for the victim. Emotional bullying can include isolation, rejection, ignoring, spreading rumors, manipulating others to cause rejection of someone and setting someone up for public embarrassment. Girls are more likely than boys to use emotional bullying against their victims.

Physical bullying includes hitting, kicking, pushing, slapping, spitting, tripping, choking, taking or defacing property and physical acts that demean and humiliate. This form of bullying is more common among boys.

Harassment is bullying that involves threats, extortion, coercion, challenging you to do something you don't want to do and ethnic, racial, religious and sexual taunting. **Sexual Harassment** is a specific form of harassment directed toward a person's sexual identity or behavior. Sexual harassment can be physical, verbal, or emotional. It can include exhibitionism, voyeurism, propositions, suggestions, sexual gestures and spreading rumors. Girls are more emotionally distressed by this form of bullying than are boys. (See information on sexual harassment in the introduction of this book.)

Where is the bullying occurring?
Before you begin addressing the problem of bullying, you need to know where exactly it is happening. Every school has areas of its campus in which students are more vulnerable to bullying due to less supervision and structure. Once you have identified where bullying is taking place on your campus, you can develop strategies that will address the problem. Administrators may want to address bullying problems in some areas of the campus by improving supervision and/or installing surveillance cameras in those spots. In other settings, instruction on the effects of bullying and creating a more positive climate might prove more helpful.

Classroom – While the classroom should be the safest place for students, bullying there still continues. When I surveyed the eighth-grade students at Sanford Middle School in Alabama, 25% of the girls and only 1% of the boys reported having been bullied in the classroom. Girls' use of emotional bullying is often so subtle that it goes under the teacher's radar. Teachers must be in the classroom at all times and try to be aware of the subtle behaviors of students.

Hall/Lockers – Because halls are often poorly supervised and overcrowded during class-changes, this is an especially vulnerable place for many students. Bumps and shoves can easily be described as "an accident" by the bully and verbal bullying can go unheard by school staff.

Outside the building – Many campuses have multiple buildings with hard-to-view passageways between them. These areas of the campus that are poorly supervised provide opportunities for bullies to attack their victims unseen by school personnel. Administration should consider safety when planning new construction on school sites.

Physical education/Locker room – Physical Education classes often require teachers to supervise more students than in any other school setting. Students often have more mobility. The less-athletically-skilled students can easily become the target of verbal and physical attacks. Some of the most serious bullying can occur in unsupervised locker rooms.

Playground – Some elementary and middle schools still allow free-play activities on a playground. Teachers must carefully supervise all playground actions, noticing who is participating and who is being left out. A playground can turn into Lord of the Flies in a matter of seconds.

Restrooms – Restrooms continue to be a very vulnerable area for bullying, smoking, vandalism and other detestable acts. Very few teachers are eager to sign up for restroom supervision, and cameras are not an option. Bureau of Justice Statistics reported that 43% of students surveyed feared harassment in the restrooms at school.

Lunchroom – For many students, lunch is the most difficult time of the school day. Tables are suddenly full or places are being saved. While I am not in favor of assigned seats in the lunchroom, bullies should not be allowed to reign in the cafeteria. Lunchroom personnel should be included in planning and training for your anti-bullying program.

School bus – Schools are just as responsible for dealing with bullying on their buses as they are in the classroom. While bus drivers should not have to be distracted from their driving to continually look in their rear-view mirrors to monitor disruptive students, they must work to prevent bullying on the bus. Having students of mixed ages on the same bus tends to increase the risk of bullying on buses.

The walk to and from School – While schools are not held legally responsible for students' welfare before they enter or after they leave school grounds; off-campus bullying does affect what happens while school is in session. Reports of bullying by students off school grounds should be addressed by the school, and the school should work cooperatively with the parents to develop a plan of action. (Unit Three - *Skills for Parents*, Unit Five - *Skills for the Bullied*)

The Internet and other electronic media – High-tech bullying is on the rise. Students can no longer be safe from bullying in their homes. The phone, Internet and text messaging, makes students vulnerable to bullying in new ways. If electronic bullying is identified as a problem among your students, the school needs to include online bullying in its anti-bullying policy and discussions.

How do students feel about the bullying?

This information can be gained through a survey, or through individual interviews or classroom discussions. It is important that students feel able to report their concerns openly and honestly. While classroom discussion may inhibit some students from sharing their feelings, an open discussion can help make all students aware that they are not the only ones distressed by bullying. Being able to discuss bullying in a protected classroom setting can be very therapeutic for students.

How serious is the problem?

Identifying what students feel are the most serious bullying problems will give you a good place to start in designing your anti-bullying program.

What do students think would help?

Always ask the students for their suggestions. Because they are the most directly affected by bullying, they often come up with the best solutions. When students identify strategies, they take more ownership in the success of the program and they can feel added satisfaction by becoming part of the solution.

How do students feel about the way adults respond to bullying?

While this is a difficult question for school to address, it is important. Most students do not believe educators are committed to stopping bullying and think the strategies teachers use are ineffective. In a 2000 survey of students who reported being bullied in the past 30 days at a middle school in Alabama, 89% of the students reported that they were not pleased with the way school officials handled the bullying situation.

COLLECTING DATA ON BULLYING
From Parents and Teachers

There are a variety of ways to collect data concerning bullying on your campus. To gain a broad understanding of bullying, students, parents and staff can be interviewed, complete surveys, and/or staff can record direct observations of student interactions. To get a complete picture of you school, you will need input from as many people as possible. One of the most effective measures of evaluating the problem of bullying is the self-administered survey completed anonymously by students, teachers and parents. You can develop a questionnaire for your school to use or adapt the ones provided in this book. The survey should be completed after the people being surveyed have been educated on the definition of bullying (Activities 1.1 *What Is Bullying?* & 1.2 *Style of Bullying.*) Everyone should be made to realize that bullying is more than hitting. Teachers and parents should be surveyed prior to the release of any student survey information.

If you are using the surveys included in this book, the following will help you analyze your results. The School Bullying Survey For Parent and Teacher can be used to survey everyone or just a sample of each population. If you are conducting a random sampling of parents or teachers, be sure to sample people in each grade level and that represent every ethnic and racial group.

One of the main goals of surveying parents and teachers is to compare what they are seeing to what students are reporting.

Teacher/Parent – You will want to analyze your statistics separately for parents and teachers. It will be interesting to see if one group is more in tuned with what students are seeing.

Grade(s) – It will be interesting to learn if bullying is different in different grades.

Question 1 – This question can be compared to question 3 on the student survey.

Style of Bullying – The ranking of parents and teachers can be compared to the student responses to questions 5-10.

Where Bullying Occurs – Compare parent and teacher responses with student responses to question 11 on the student survey.

Electronic Bullying – Because electronic bullying is relatively new, this can be an opportunity for school to gather additional information about the problem.

Questions 2-8 – The answers to these questions can be compared to student questions 15-21. It is important for parents and teachers to realize their awareness or lack of awareness to the problem of bullying.

School Bullying Survey (Parents and Teachers)

Parents and teachers, please answer the following questions based on observations and experiences you have had in our school and with our students. Use the following definition of bullying to answer the questions.

Bullying is any repeated, intentional act by a more powerful person, which causes embarrassment, pain or discomfort.

❑ Parent   ❑ Teacher   Grade(s) you teach/your child's grade(s) _____

1. Have you seen or heard of incidents of bullying at this school during the past month?
   ❑ Yes   ❑ No

   Based on what you have seen and heard, rank these types of bullying from one to six based on their frequency. One would be the most frequent type of bullying and six would be the least frequent.

   _____ teasing
   _____ name calling
   _____ threatening or intimidation
   _____ being excluded or left out
   _____ hitting, pushing or kicking
   _____ unwelcome sexual comments, gestures or touching

   Put an X by the three places where you feel bullying is most likely to occur at our school

   _____ On the school bus   _____ In the restroom
   _____ In the halls/at lockers   _____ In the classroom
   _____ At P.E. or on the playground   _____ In the locker room
   _____ On the Internet or phone   _____ In the lunchroom
   _____ Walking to or from school   Other _____
   _____ Walking between buildings   _____

   Parents – If your child has been the victim of electronic bullying (phone or Internet); please describe the incident(s).

   _____

   _____

   _____

   _____

   _____

   _____

   _____

School Bullying Survey (continued)
(Parents and Teachers)

Circle your answer to the following questions.

2. Overall, how would you rank the problem of bullying at school?

   Intolerable   Irritating   No Problem

3. How well do adults deal with bullying at school?

   Well   Adequately   Poorly

4. Do you feel students are safe from bullies at school?

   Yes   No   Unsure

5. Do you think bullies are admired or liked at school?

   Yes   No   Unsure

6. Do you think students know how to report bullying?

   Yes   No   Unsure

7. Are students willing to report bullying problems to school officials?

   Yes   No   Unsure

8. Have you yourself used bullying behavior with students/your child(ren) as a means of discipline? (Please review the definition on the previous page.)

   Rarely   Occasionally   Often

Please write down any additional information, comments or suggestions that you feel will help our school improve in the way we treat one another.

_____

_____

_____

_____

_____

_____

_____

_____

_____

COLLECTING DATA ON BULLYING
From Students

If you are using the *School Bullying Survey For Students*, included in this book, the following will help you analyze your results.

Introduction – You may want to adapt the introductory statement to reflect your school's approach to bullying. If you commit to doing something about problems that are identified in the survey, be sure to follow through.

Definition – You may want to use the definition developed from activity 1.1 *What is Bullying?* on your survey, or you can use the definition that is provided. Whichever option you choose, make sure the students have a working definition of bullying

Males/Females – You will want to analyze the results for your girls and boys separately as well as together. The statistics will likely be significantly different on some questions for males and females.

Age/Grade – Statistics may be different for students who are not the same age as others in their grade. You may also see significant differences between grades themselves.

Questions 1 - 4 will give you the percentage of students in your school who have ever been bullied.

Questions 5 - 10 will give you a picture of the types and frequency of bullying during the previous 30 days. I do not recommend having students complete a survey during the first 30 days of the school year. You may not get an accurate picture of the bullying problem during the first month of school. This survey begins with less-serious forms of bullying (teasing) and progresses to more-serious types(hitting, etc.).

Question 11 will help you identify where bullying is taking place on your campus. You may want to adjust the list to reflect your school's needs.

Questions 12-15 are only answered by students who have been bullied during the last month. These questions give information on the students' feelings concerning the staff's awareness of and response to the problem of bullying.

Questions 15 – 20 are designed to get some interesting information on how students feel about the issue related to bullying. The answers to these questions can be important to determine the overall climate of the school.

Question 15 gives you an idea of the intensity of the problem at your school.

Question 16 gives you an overall student rating of adult responses to bullying.

Question 17 will give you a good idea of the extent of the problem on your campus. Restoring a feeling of safety is critical to students' emotional and academic well-being.

Question 18 lets you know the attitude toward bullies on your campus. If your students admire the bullies; you will need to use specific strategies to help them understand why bullying is wrong.

Question 19 reveals if the students know how to report bullying on your campus.

Question 20 indicates the level of trust the students have in the ability of the staff. Students will not report bullying if they feel nothing will be done in response to their report or that their identity will not be protected and the bully might retaliate against them for reporting.

Question 21 was added to see if after addressing bullying in a survey, students might be able to identify some of their own behaviors as bullying. Self-evaluation is important when addressing bullying. I found the results interesting at my school and I think you will too.

You will want to encourage students to write comments or suggestions of their own on the survey.

SCHOOL BULLYING SURVEY
(Students)

Activity 1.1

Purpose
Gather information on bullying from students.
To help students feel their input is important and that they can contribute to the solution.

Materials
Student handout - *School Bullying Survey*

Procedures
Give each student a copy of the **School Bullying Survey**. Read the introduction to the class or have a student read it aloud and discuss the statement with the students.

Read the definition of bullying to the students. Tell students that a bully is a person who is trying to make himself feel more powerful. Bullies often look for someone they feel has less power than they do. A person can be more powerful physically, socially, economically or by virtue of age. Encourage students to take this survey seriously. The results are important to the school, and therefore, it is important to each of them. Remind them that no one will know who completed the survey and instruct all students not to look at the surveys of those around them. Have students complete the survey. If students are not good readers, you may want to read each question aloud and have all students answer at the same time. Allow plenty of time for students to write their comments or suggestions on the survey.

Take up the survey as soon as they are completed to avoid having students see the answers of others.

Follow-up
Ask the students:
- What have you learned about bullying from completing this survey?
- What do you think will be identified as the most serious problems?
- What are some suggestions you have for dealing with the problem of bullying?

School Bullying Survey

We want our school to be a better place to learn and live. Please answer the following questions about the way people behave toward one another in our school. By answering these questions, you are helping us learn about problems our school might have. If problems are identified, something will be done to improve the situation. Please answer honestly we want to know how you feel. No one will know your name. Use the following definition to answer the questions.

Bullying is any repeated, intentional act by a more powerful person, which causes you embarrassment, pain or discomfort.

(Check one) ❑ Male ❑ Female   Age _____ Grade _____

Check your answer.

1. Have you ever been bullied at this school or any school?
   ❑ Yes   ❑ No

2. Have you been bullied at this school during the past year?
   ❑ Yes   ❑ No

3. Have you been bullied at this school during the past month?
   ❑ Yes   ❑ No

4. Have you been bullied at this school during the past week?
   ❑ Yes   ❑ No

Answer the following questions based on your experiences during the past 30 days.

5. How many times have you been teased in a way that made you feel uncomfortable?
   0   1-2   3-4   more than 4

6. How many times have you been called names by others?
   0   1-2   3-4   more than 4

7. How many times have you been threatened or intimidated by others?
   0   1-2   3-4   more than 4

8. How many times have you been excluded or left out on purpose?
   0   1-2   3-4   more than 4

9. How many times have you been hit, pushed or kicked?
   0   1-2   3-4   more than 4

10. How many times have you experienced unwelcome sexual comments, gestures or touching?
    0   1-2   3-4   more than 4

School Bullying Survey *(continued)*

11. Put an X by each place where you have been bullied during the past month.

_____ On the school bus   _____ In the restroom
_____ In the halls/at lockers   _____ In the classroom
_____ At P.E. or on the playground   _____ In the locker room
_____ On the Internet or phone   _____ In the lunchroom
_____ Walking to or from school   Other _____
_____ Walking between buildings   _____

If you have been bullied during the past 30 days, answer questions 12-14.
If not, skip ahead to # 15.

12. The bullying I received was from ....
   ❑ Boys   ❑ Girls   ❑ Boys & Girls   ❑ Younger   ❑ Older   ❑ Same Age

13. Were school officials aware of the bullying?
   ❑ Yes   ❑ No

14. If yes, were you pleased with the way school officials handled the bullying situation?
   ❑ Yes   ❑ No

All students answer the following questions.

15. Overall, how much of a problem is bullying at school?
   ❑ Intolerable   ❑ Irritating   ❑ No Problem

16. How well do adults deal with bullying at our school?
   ❑ Well   ❑ Adequately   ❑ Poorly

17. Do you feel safe from bullies at our school?
   ❑ Yes   ❑ No

18. Do you admire or like bullies?
   ❑ Yes   ❑ No

19. Do you know how to report bullying?
   ❑ Yes   ❑ No

20. Would you be willing to report bullying problems to school officials?
   ❑ Yes   ❑ No

21. Have you yourself bullied another student during the past 30 days?
   ❑ Yes   ❑ No

Please write down any additional information, comments or suggestions that you feel will help our school improve in the way we treat one another.

_____

_____

SCHOOL SAFETY SURVEY

Activity 1.2

Purpose
To determine students needs for safety.

Materials
Student handout – **School Safety Survey** or similar survey adapted to the needs of the individual school. Many schools have already implemented many of the items listed on this survey. You will want to delete items that are already in place at your school and perhaps add other issues that need to be addressed.

Procedure
Tell the students that in order to provide a safer learning environment, the school wants to identify safety concerns of its students. The responses from the **School Safety Surveys** will be used to provide information for the school, so staff can identify the best ways to devote their energy and resources. Students can include their names if they feel comfortable. If they include their name, they may be interviewed at a later time to provide more feedback on safety issues.

Remind students that these surveys are confidential. Have students complete the survey and collect them.

Follow-up
Ask the Students:
- Do we all have the same need for safety?
- Are you concerned that some of these measures would violate your right to privacy?
- Can we ever do too much to make our school safe?

SCHOOL SAFETY SURVEY

Name (Optional)_____ Grade _____

We want to create a safe environment in which you can learn. Please complete this survey. This information will be used to help improve the safety of all students. Put an "X" beside the responses that you feel would make our school and campus safer.

I would feel safer at school if:

_____ We carried see-through book bags.

_____ We wore uniforms.

_____ Outside doors were locked at all times.

_____ We had weekly locker checks.

_____ Lockers were in a more secure area.

_____ All students involved in fights were suspended.

_____ More of the disruptive students were sent to alternative schools.

_____ The principal and/or staff patrolled the halls more.

_____ There were monitors in the halls and restrooms.

_____ There were security cameras in the halls and other sites on campus.

_____ All adults wore name tags.

_____ We had security guards on campus.

_____ There was a fence around the school campus.

_____ We practiced emergency drills more often.

_____ People entering the school were screened with metal detectors.

Other _____

Check if this statement is true for you.

_____ I do not feel safe at school.

If you checked that you do not feel safe at school, respond to the other statements by checking the ones that are true or add your own response.

I do not feel safe because:

_____ Of the school violence that has been reported in the news in recent years.

_____ I am concerned that someone will bother my possessions.

_____ I am concerned that someone will hit or push me.

_____ I have had a serious threat made against me by another student.

_____ I am afraid that students will bring weapons to school to hurt other students.

Other _____

ANTI-BULLYING POLICY

Our school does not tolerate bullying in any form. All members of the school community are committed to ensuring a physically and emotionally safe environment. We strive to value the rights of all people to learn without fear.

Bullying is any repeated, intentional act by a more powerful person that causes others embarrassment, pain or discomfort.

- Bullying can take a number of forms, including physical, verbal and emotional.
- Bullying is an abuse of power.
- Bullying shows disrespect for the worth of others.
- Bullying can be perpetrated by individuals or groups.

Examples of bullying include:

- All forms of physical violence, such as hitting, pushing, choking, tripping or spitting;
- Disturbing another person's property with the intention of stealing, hiding, damaging or destroying it;
- Inappropriate teasing, name-calling or spreading rumors about others or their families;
- Showing disrespect for others abilities and achievements;
- Writing offensive comments or graffiti about others;
- Making disparaging remarks about another's culture, religion or economic and/or social status;
- Excluding others from a group in an intentional and insensitive way;
- Encouraging others to do something that is inappropriate, dangerous or immoral;
- Making sexually suggestive comments or engaging in other forms of sexual harassment;
- Making fun of another person's clothing or physical appearance;
- Using threats to force others to act in inappropriate ways against their will;
- Using e-mail, phone or other electronic means to send hurtful messages;

The consequences of being bullied.

- You may feel frightened, embarrassed, angry or mistreated.
- You may have difficulty completing your work, experience problems concentrating, and lose interest in activities you once enjoyed.
- You may find yourself withdrawing from your family and friends.
- You may feel confused and not know what to do about the problem.

How will we prevent bullying at our school?

As a caring school community, we make a commitment to intervene if we can do so safely. We will not allow cases of bullying to go unreported. Everyone's safety is everyone's responsibility.

To ensure that bullying is stopped, the administrators' responsibilities are to:

- Provide moral leadership for the school and demonstrate respect for all students and staff;
- Remain visible on the campus and available to everyone;
- Be fair and consistent in the enforcement of the discipline policy;
- Afford students who violate the discipline policies opportunities to learn the correct behavior and acquire new skills;
- Take all reports of bullying seriously, investigate allegations and provide follow-up;
- Ensure everyone is safe by providing needed supervision and appropriate security measures on campus.

To ensure that bullying is stopped, the teachers' and staffs' responsibilities are to:

- Serve as role models at all times by demonstrating a high level of respect for all students;
- Provide a classroom environment that is safe for students to learn and develop self-esteem;
- Be vigilant in looking for signs of distress or suspected incidents of bullying;
- Provide the necessary supervision on the campus and hallways as well as in the classroom to ensure safety from bullying;
- Keep the class supervised at all times and move promptly between lessons;
- Have a structured activity planned during transition times.
- Find ways to respond to victims in less-obvious ways that will not place the victim at additional risk;
- Respond promptly when bullying behaviors are observed and follow up to make sure the bullying has not continued.

To ensure that bullying is stopped, the students' responsibilities are to:

- Refuse to participate in any bullying situation.
- Report all incidents or suspected incidents of bullying to the administration or staff.
- Refuse to protect bullies by keeping silent when they know what the bullies are doing is wrong.
- Take some action to stop the bullying if it can be done without physical risk.

To ensure that bullying is stopped, the school recommends that parents:

- Talk with their children every day and listen to their feelings;
- Be aware of signs of distress in their children, such as a sudden desire to stay home from school, unexplained headaches, missing or damaged possessions, requests for extra money or suspicious bruising;
- Get to know their children's friends and take an active interest their social life;
- Encourage their child to report any incidents of bullying to school staff; (When children take responsibility for reporting incidents of bullying, they are taking a step toward solving their own problems.)
- Keep a written record of suspected bullying incidents (who, what, when, where, why, how) to provide to the school when making a report.
- Do not encourage their child to retaliate by becoming violent with the bully;
- Keep the school informed concerning cases of suspected bullying, even if it does not involve the parent's own child.

PHYSICAL MODIFICATIONS AND INCREASED SUPERVISION

The physical environment does not cause bullying, but it may make bullying more or less likely to occur. The Center for Disease Control report that was published in 2001, found that 50% of all school-associated violent deaths occurred during transition times during the school day. Most schools report that violence and bullying greatly decrease when playgrounds, restrooms, lunchrooms and other problem areas are properly monitored. Increasing positive supervision and interaction with the students is the goal. If students feel the supervision is of an "I'm going to get you" nature, you may have negative responses from the students.

To reduce the risk of bullying at your school:

- Reduce overcrowding in the school, hallways and classrooms;
- Ensure that all classrooms have two-way communication systems;
- Provide good lighting and accessibility to all areas of the campus;
- Install surveillance equipment in hallways, between buildings, in the lunchroom and on the buses;
- Require teachers to effectively supervise their classroom during instruction time.
- Encourage teachers to use enriching lessons to keep students attention on instruction;
- Call for teachers to stand in their door-ways to supervise both the hall and their classroom during class changes and locker time.
- Supply additional staff if available in the halls during class changes and locker time;
- Conduct random searches of book bags and lockers;
- Remove all lockers from the school. When students are issued text-books, they are to take the books home for use with homework. Teachers will provide a classroom set of text-books for in school assignments or reference. If students do not have to carry text books from class to class they will no longer need book bags or lockers;
- Stagger class changes so fewer students are in the hall at one time;
- Supply male and female staff for supervision of restrooms and changing areas for PE;
- Train students as "safety buddies." These students could be asked accompany certain vulnerable students to the restroom or locker areas.

Seldom is it a good idea to have students serve as hall or restroom monitors. While you want to encourage all students to report inappropriate behavior to the school staff, having students serve as monitors can put them in the difficult position of **having** to tell on their peers. Student monitors could be intimidated by bullies into not reporting incidents, or you could inadvertently create a little "Gestapo" of "student monitors" who abuse their power and use it to strike fear into the hearts of other students. The kinds of students who can handle this responsibility are few and far between. However, implementing a peer helper program can help prevent bullying situations from escalating or even starting. While we want to encourage students to report bullying or violent behaviors to the staff, creating an organized group can sometimes lead to additional problems.

REPORTING BULLYING BEHAVIOR

Because most bullying goes unobserved by the teachers and staff, it is critical that the administration encourage reporting and make reporting an easy and safe process. The administration and staff cannot deal with problems they are not aware of. Many schools have established a hotline where anyone can call and make reports of dangerous or inappropriate behavior.

STUDENT REPORTS

For students to be willing to report bullying of themselves or others, they must feel that they will be taken seriously and that their identity will be protected. A Washington Post article reported that two-thirds of bullying victims didn't believe that the bully would be dealt with appropriately, so many were reluctant to report it. When a student reports being bullied, it is very likely that he/she is telling the truth. Most victims feel humiliated for being bullied and even more so for having to ask for help. Many suffer in silence because experience has taught them that reporting doesn't help and can even make matters worse. They begin to buy into the lie that bullying is a necessary part of growing up and that adults are not willing to help them.

To increase reporting:

- Have a clear policy and procedure for reporting bullying and make sure all students are familiar with the process;
- Assure the confidentiality of the reported;
- Provide a drop box where reports can be made anonymously; (Ex. "Schools Concerns")
- Take all reports seriously;
- Listen carefully to the victim; (You may occasionally have a student who simply wants to get someone else in trouble.)
- Ask the victim what he/she thinks will help the situation;
- Evaluate the needs of the victim and offer skills training *(Unit Six, Skills for The Victim)*;
- Evaluate the motivation of the bully and offer skills training *(Unit Five, Skills for the Bully)*;
- Keep a record of bullying and intervention strategies that have been used;
- Check back with the victim to see if the intervention has helped;
- Check back with the victim again to see if the interventions are still helping.

TEACHER/STAFF REPORTS

Teachers and staff need to feel empowered with skills to deal with bullies and know they will have the support of the administration when they address a bullying situation in their classrooms or any area on campus. The administration needs to have clear guidelines concerning when and how teachers and staff should make reports to the administration. Students need to be aware that all staff have the authority to intervene when they become aware of inappropriate behavior.

All staff need to:

- Stop all bullying behavior immediately when you see it;
- Try to protect the feelings of the victim;
- Talk to the involved parties separately and in private;
- Try to determine factors leading up to the incident;
- Consider what you know about the prior relationship of the students and each student's personality;
- Keep a record of all bullying incidents and strategies you have used;
- Report all incidents that you feel need further investigation to the administration.

PARENT REPORTS

Parents need to feel their reports will be taken seriously and that the school authorities will take appropriate action and protect their child from additional trauma. Parents are often reluctant to tell others about their child's problems. By the time a parent comes to the school for help, the child has often endured significant distress.

To gain parent support:

- Inform all parents of the school's policy on bullying;
- Communicate a willingness by the school to work with parents regarding problems of bullying;
- Listen to the parent's concerns and be sensitive to the strong emotions parents will often have concerning their child;
- Gather as much information as you can from the parents (Who, what, when, where, how often, etc.);
- Try to identify other students who may have additional information concerning the incident(s);
- Ask the parents for suggestions on what they, or their child thinks would help;
- Within limits of confidentiality, keep the parent informed regarding the school's response;
- Check back with the parents or ask them to report on the effectiveness of the school's response.

EVALUATING REPORTS OF BULLYING

All reports of bullying must be taken seriously if you want students to continue to make them. Investigating bullying can take a great deal of time. Often school staff must make decisions concerning the seriousness of the offense and the time it will take to investigate the incident. It is often better to spend the time resolving the conflict between the students than investigating to determine exactly what happened. It is not always necessary to establish who is to "blame" if we can instead begin the process of reconciliation between the students.

Some reports of bullying can be handled by:

- Providing the students with an opportunity to go to mediation;
- Having the students mutually agree to stop the behavior and/or stay away from each other;
- Allowing the students to sign a behavioral contract. *(Behavioral Contracts)*.

Certainly there are serious and/or chronic cases of bullying that need investigation. The more sources that provide collaborating evidence, the more confident you can be of what is taking place. Chronic bullying and/or violent behaviors need an increasing level of response and more-serious consequences for the bully.

ASSESSING THE SERIOUSNESS OF BULLYING

The level of distress of the victim is one of the most critical factors in determining the seriousness of the bullying. Remember that we are all hurt by different things. When a person continues to call you "nerd" after he/she knows it distresses you, this can constitute serious bullying. The more chronic the incidents of bullying and a lack of empathy by the bully, also elevate the seriousness of the situation.

In assessing the seriousness of bullying, find out the answer to these questions.

- How distressed is the victim?
- How many incidents of bullying have occurred between these students?
- How long has the bullying behavior been going on?
- Was there violence or a threat of future violence?
- Was the bully's intention to harm the victim?
- Does the bully exhibit any empathy for the victim?
- Does the bully display remorse for his/her behavior?
- Is the bully willing to accept responsibility for his/her behavior and resolve the problem?

STUDENT REPORTING POLICY

Every school needs to develop a policy for students to make reports of bullying, violence or other dangerous activities.

The Code of Silence

One of the greatest barriers for student reports is the "code of silence" that exists between the students and staff. Students are not supposed to "tell on" each other. There is often a "them against us" mentality among the students that is often hard to break down. During the education phase of the anti-bullying campaign it is important to break this barrier down and encourage students to help take part in their own safety. Everyone's safety is everyone's problem. The administration must have as many students on their side as they can get.

Tattling vs. Reporting

Teachers often discourage students from tattling on each other. It is important to distinguish between tattling and reporting. The difference between the two is in your intention. With tattling, your intention is to get someone in trouble. The intention with reporting is to keep someone safe. If someone is in danger of being hurt physically or emotionally, students need to make a report to a school staff member.

Who do you tell?

Students should be encouraged to report bullying or other inappropriate behaviors to the staff member who has authority over them at the time when the behavior occurred. This person is usually the teacher. It is very important that the teacher establish a level of trust with his/her students to facilitate this reporting. There should also be at least one, and in larger schools several, school staff members whom any student can make reports of bullying to. This should preferably be a person who is never responsible for disciplining students. The staff member who is identified for receiving reports of bullying, should make a statement to the entire student body on several occasions that his/her door is always open to students with concerns about safety or personal concerns. Every effort should be made to allow flexible time for at least one staff member to listen to student concerns.

Don't tell I told!

When a student makes a serious report, every effort should be made to protect his/her identity. Several other students can be questioned before and after the reporting to camouflage the identity of the reporter. If you want to continue to get reports from students they must feel safe from retaliation from other students.

DEVELOPING DISCIPLINE POLICIES

When students, parents and staff are involved in developing discipline policies and/or anti-bullying policies, they experience a sense of ownership and often take more responsibility for their behavior.

PARTICIPANTS
- **Staff** members can be identified to participate who reflect the various grade levels on your campus and represent the diversity of student needs.
- **Student** leaders who have been identified through school elections (Student Council officers or members, club or class officers, etc.) should be invited to participate and provide input. Student participation should reflect the racial and ethnic diversity of the student body.
- **Parent** volunteers and parents who serve in leadership in parent-teacher organizations and are familiar with the day-to-day operation of the school, should also to be invited. Be sure to consider the racial and ethnic diversity of the school when seeking parent participants.

PURPOSE
Because policy development is a mammoth job, it is probably not advisable to begin this process with a blank page. Make sure the task of the group is clearly explained to all participants from the beginning. Tasks might include:

- Reviewing student and staff surveys concerning bullying and/or safety;
- Reviewing current policies and making suggestions;
- Evaluating current consequences for violations and the appropriateness of the consequences;
- Identifying additional consequences for violation of policies;
- Exploring the need for new policies. (Dress code, bullying, sexual harassment, Internet use, cell phones, etc.)

GROUND RULES
- All policies should address a problem or prevent a problem.
- All policies should help reach one of the following goals.
  Keep students safe,
  Help students learn,
  Help students get along.

LEADERSHIP
- It is probably best that school personnel moderate the process of policy development.
- The leader should have a clear vision for the process and communicate that vision to all participants.
- Everyone needs to understand the authority of the group. (Is the group making policy or will its product be submitted to a higher authority for consideration?)
- Identify a timeline for the process and keep the group on task.

PROCESS

- Because you are including students, staff and parents it is important that this diverse group have a chance to get to know one another. Select one (or more) of the get acquainted activities found in *Unit two, Skills for Teachers* to get the group talking and sharing.
- Identify the goal of the group and clearly identify the parameters.
- The leader may choose to divide the group into smaller units to problem-solve and bring their group product back to the larger group. (Small groups should each represent the diversity of the larger group.)
- Periodically evaluate progress.
- Use group problem solving *(Activities 4.14, 15, & 16)* to facilitate process.
- Encourage all participants to share their input.
- Respect all suggestions.
- Continue to combine and reword your product until the group is reasonably in agreement.

SCHOOL RESPONSE TO THREATS: EXPECT THE BEST, BE PREPARED FOR THE WORST

Adolescent violence in general and homicides in particular, have decreased since 1993 according to the Centers for Disease Control and Prevention. "The risk of violent death that a child faces at school is less than one in a million," says Mark Anderson, an epidemiologist with the CDC. This encouraging statistic seemed of little importance when the massacre at Columbine High School in Littleton, CO in April 1999 forced the nation to take another look at the safety of our schools. However, schools must **avoid overreacting** with inflexible policies.

Understanding violence after it has occurred is difficult, but trying to assess a threat and keep it from being carried out is even more challenging. Schools need to focus on **proactive strategies** to identify students who need our help and then get them the help they need. That being said, schools must react quickly and appropriately to threats of violence by students. In 1999, after the Columbine shootings, the *National Center for the Analysis of Violent Crime* **(NCAVC)** issued a report entitled *The School Shooter: A Threat Assessment Perspective*. This report gives schools some guidelines for assessing the seriousness of a student-made threat. High-quality threat assessment can help the school avoid overreacting to less-serious threats and unfairly punishing a student who is not dangerous or under-reacting to a serious threat.

Threat –

an expression of intent to do harm or act out violently against someone or something. A threat can be spoken, written or implied. A threat may be a warning signal or a cry for help.

- All threats should be taken seriously and assessed. Whether the threat is **direct** ("I placed a bomb in the cafeteria."); **indirect** ("I could kill you if I wanted to."); **veiled** ("This school would be better off without you.") or **conditional** ("If you do that again, I'm going to kill you.") the threat should be assessed.

- Most students who make threats are unlikely to carry them out. The roots of violence are usually very complicated. Students come to school with a collective experience shaped by the family environment, school, peers, community and culture. While no one factor creates a violent student, every factor has its effects.

ASSESSING A THREAT

The National Center for the Analysis of Violent Crime recommends that school authorities examine the following factors when assessing the seriousness of a student made threat.

Motivation –
Understanding motive is a key element of evaluating a threat. Is the threat a warning signal, demand for attention, assertion of power, effort to frighten or terrorize, attempt to strike back for an injury or injustice, to test authority, or to protect oneself?

Emotion –
Are the emotions underlying the threat those of love, hate, fear, rage or the desire for attention, revenge, excitement or recognition? The more emotionally charged threats may sound frightening, but no correlation has been established between the emotional intensity in a threat and the risk that it will be carried out.

Precipitating Factors –
What was the student's state of mind when the threat was made? Alcohol or drugs can have a strong, temporary influence. Look for incidents of romantic breakup, failing grades, isolation, victimization, conflict with peers or conflict with a parent in the life of the student making the threat. Once the shock of these incidents has passed, the likelihood of violence may also have diminished.

Plausibility –
Is the threat specific, identifying plausible details? Details can include the identity of the victim(s), reason for making the threat, weapon to be used, or the time and place the threat will be carried out. Specific details can indicate that thought, planning and preparations have already been made, suggesting a higher risk of follow-through. Details that are specific but not logical or plausible usually indicate a less-serious threat.

High Level of Threat:
A threat that appears to pose an imminent and serious danger to the safety of others. A threat that is assessed as high-level will almost always require **immediate law-enforcement intervention**.

A high-level threat is one that:

- Is direct, specific and plausible;
- Suggests that concrete steps have already been taken toward carrying it out;
- Comes in conjunction with high risk factors in major areas of the student's life.

ASSESSING HIGH RISK FACTORS FOR STUDENTS

The *NCAVC* report concluded that the more information available about the student(s) making the threat, the more accurate the assessment will be. The following four aspects of the student's life should be evaluated.

- **Personality of the student –**
  How well does he cope with anger and disappointments? How does the student feel about himself and what is his response to others?

- **Family dynamic –**
  What are the patterns of behavior in the family? Is there a history of violence and a lack of adherence to societal norms within the family?

- **School dynamic and the student's role in that dynamic –**
  Do certain students get more approval and attention from school authorities? How well do the students see themselves fitting in with the school's value system?

- **Social dynamic –**
  Who are the student's friends, what activities does he participate in, what is the student's preferred reading material, what is his/her attitude toward drugs, alcohol and violence?

If the student appears to have serious problems in a majority of these four life areas and if the threat is assessed as high-level, the threat should be taken more seriously, and appropriate intervention by school and law enforcement authorities should be quickly initiated.

SCHOOL DYNAMICS

All four aspects of the student's life identified on the previous page should be considered when assessing the seriousness of a threat. While the school can exert some influence over all four of the areas, it has the most influence over the area of school dynamics. Schools need to examine the seven areas of school dynamics that are identified in the NCAVC report to determine the degree of positive or negative influence the school is having on a potentially violent student.

Among the issues to be examined for student violence are:

- **The Student's Attachment to School –**
  Students who appear to be detached from school, other students, teachers and school activities are more at risk for violence. Students who participate in clubs and school activities and have friendships and positive relationships with teachers are at a reduced risk for violence;

- **Tolerance for Disrespectful Behavior –**
  If the school does little to prevent or punish disrespectful behavior between individual students, the risk of student violence increases. When bullying is part of the school culture and school authorities seem oblivious to it, anger and resentment flourish;

- **Inequitable Discipline –**
  If discipline is inequitably applied or there is a perception that it is being inequitably applied, the risk of school violence increases;

- **Inflexible Culture –**
  When the patterns of behavior, values and relationships are static, unyielding and insensitive to changes in society, students can feel more of a need to rebel to have their needs heard;

- **Pecking Order Among Students –**
  Threats can increase when certain groups of students are given or appear to be given more prestige and respect in the school;

- **Code of Silence –**
  For students to report potential threats, they must feel that they can safely tell teachers or administrators about their concern and feel they will be taken seriously. The more trust the students have for the school staff the more likely they are to report dangers;

- **Unsupervised Computer Access –**
  If students are able to use the school's computers to play violent computer games or to explore inappropriate Web sites, the potential for inappropriate behavior by the students increases.

PROMOTE EQUITY AND RESPECT

Schools must be more deliberate in the promotion of positive social values among students. To promote equity and respect schools need to:

Adopt a policy of respect.

Respect should be the foundation of all our communication and interactions. We acknowledge the dignity and worth of one another, and endeavor to in no way diminish another by our conduct or our attitudes.

Ensure respect for student's religion, gender, nationality, and sexual preference.

The school is obligated to protect students under federal, state and local laws. Create a positive school climate that fosters acceptance and tolerance for differences.

Provide instruction on diversity.

Encourage teachers to create opportunities for students of diverse backgrounds to share information with the class concerning their nationality or religion. Highlight individuals in diverse cultures with positive character traits. Help students get to know each other and appreciate each other. (Activities 2.1, 2, 3, 4 & 5, 4.17)

Take all reports of discrimination seriously.

Provide a means of reporting complaints of bullying or discrimination to specific personnel. Make students aware of who these contacts are and that their reporting will be kept confidential.

Ensure that all staff model an attitude of acceptance for diversity.

Teachers have a special responsibility to search within themselves for their biases and do everything they can to eliminate them. They have a responsibility to intervene whenever the attitudes or actions of a student or staff member jeopardize the dignity or welfare of any student.

Respond strongly to all incidents of hate, bullying or prejudice.

The school must denounce any hateful act and address the fears and confusion that result.

MIX IT UP AT LUNCH DAY

Breaking down social boundaries among students can be difficult. These boundaries create division and misunderstandings in schools and communities. *Teaching Tolerance and Tolerance.org*, divisions of *The Southern Poverty Law Center* in Montgomery AL, sponsors a *National Mix it Up Day*. Each November, the Center challenges students to take the first step toward breaking down social barriers by sitting outside their usual lunch circle for a day. When the **Center** surveyed students in 2000, one third of the students said it was hard to make friends with people in different groups. When asked which boundaries were the hardest to cross, students identified these attributes in the following order:

1. Personal appearance
2. Athletic achievement
3. Style
4. Race
5. Academic achievement

When students were asked what locations they could see the boundaries the most clearly, they identified the following:

1. Cafeteria
2. Classroom
3. Bus
4. Recreational activities
5. After-school clubs

To get more information including activity booklets for early, middle and upper grades, contact the Southern Poverty Law Center, P.O. Box 548, Montgomery, AL 36104-0548.

FRIENDSHIP TEAMS

Increase your schools extracurricular opportunities by starting a **Friendship Club**. Friendship skills need to be recognized by students, staff and administration as important to the wellbeing of the overall school experience. When students have friendships and positive relationships, their achievement is enhanced and the schools experience fewer absences and a lower drop-out rate.

Students participating in this club could be given instruction on friendship skills (Unit Two - Activities 2.1, 2.2, 2.3, 2.4, 2.5, Unit Five – Activities 5.12, 5.13, and 5.14) and intervention skills (Unit Three – Activities 3.5, 3.6, 3.7, 3.8, 3.9, 3.10, 3.11, 3.12, and 3.13).

Teams of students could be identified to work together on tasks. When students have support from other students they are more likely to feel empowered and act responsibly. This club could identify numerous roles to serve throughout the school. They could:

- Volunteer to assist new students who enroll in the school;

- Perform "random acts of kindness" throughout the school;

- Assume responsibility to make sure certain students are included in activities and projects;

- Invite students who are sitting alone to join them in the lunchroom or on the play-ground;

- Intervene when they see signs of bullying;

- Sponsor school activities that promote friendship such as "Make a New Friend Day," "Share a Smile Day," etc.

OPPORTUNITIES FOR COMMUNITY SERVICE

We overwhelm children with all the suffering and evil in the world, but do we enable them to act?

– Sister Joan Magnetti

Unfortunately, students continue to witness (if only through the media) disasters, wars, atrocities and mayhem which results in widespread human suffering. Students can either feel helpless and vulnerable or they can be given opportunities to make a difference. People want to help. Schools should encourage students to respond to the needs in their community. Why did thousands of people donate blood in the days following 9-11? They wanted to do something that would help. While students cannot solve all the problems they are aware of, they can and should be encouraged to do something. When we all do something it will Make a Difference.

As a school community, we can make students aware of the needs and suffering of others in their community, country, and world. They can help organize student-action projects. Projects might include:

- Environmental projects such as planting trees, landscaping areas, litter control, planning earth day activities or programs to increase awareness of pollution, global warming, the rain forest, etc;
- Disaster relief projects where students respond to a specific disaster by collecting money or needed supplies;
- School-wide collections to assist with needs such as collecting canned foods, coats, school supplies, etc.

Schools can give students the opportunity to provide service within the school by sponsoring:

- Peer tutoring programs;
- Cross-age mentoring programs;
- Peer mediation programs;
- School spirit, clean-up, kindness, and etc. campaigns.

Make an effort to integrate community service into the academic program by encouraging:

- All clubs and organizations to sponsor service projects;
- Class or subject area to develop service learning programs related to the curriculum;
- Giving elective credit for participating in approved community volunteer programs. Students would have their volunteer program approved and provide documentation of a pre-specified number of volunteer hours. (Red Cross, local animal shelter, Boys and Girls Club, food bank, etc.)

Unit Two
Bullying in the Classroom – Skills for Teachers

BULLYING IN THE CLASSROOM: SKILLS FOR TEACHERS

"The mediocre teacher tells.

The good teacher explains.

The superior teacher demonstrates.

The great teacher inspires."

— *William Arthur Ward (1921-1997)*
American Author and Teacher

Unit Two
BULLYING IN THE CLASSROOM
SKILLS FOR TEACHERS

Teachers have a tremendous opportunity to create a positive impact on students who bully in their classroom and throughout the entire school. Because teachers spend more time working directly with students than anyone else in the school, this gives them a wonderful opportunity to exert a positive influence on students' attitudes and actions. At a time when schools are putting more and more pressure on educators to concentrate on standardized tests, teachers often look at an anti-bullying program as just one more thing they have to worry about. Protecting your students' dignity and self worth must become a priority.

Educators must first recognize the extent of the problems that bullying creates. Teachers usually underestimate the amount of bullying that takes place, and too many teachers are reluctant to get involved when they do see it. **Dan Olweus**, a professor of psychology at the **University of Bergen in Norway**, reports that there is a wide gap between the amount of bullying students report and the amount their teachers see. Many teachers feel powerless to do much about bullying. They don't know how to stop it, and some feel that they wouldn't be supported by their principals if they tried. The problem of bullying is too pervasive and damaging for educators to continue to ignore.

Educators must recognize the serious effect that bullying has on all their students. Students often report that when they tell their teachers about the bullying, the teachers frequently do not take them seriously. Teachers offer strategies such as "ignore them" or at times make the student feel responsible to go back and work the problem out on his/her own. Students do need to learn to settle conflicts, but these are skills that must be taught. Is it fair to hold students accountable for skills they have never been taught?

If all the adults within a school are committed to preventing bullying behavior, they **will make a difference**. When teachers intervene every time they see bullying behaviors, when requesting teacher intervention means that action will be taken and the power imbalance between the bully and victim is equalized, students will be safer. If all teachers in all grades are teaching caring and respect for everyone all year long, year after year, the cycle of victimization and bullying can be broken. Even if there is little support outside the school, the school can create a caring community within its walls. Teachers can work at the classroom level, and also with individual children who are victims, bullies and bystanders.

WHAT ARE YOU TEACHING?

Teachers must be more conscious of what they are teaching their students and more deliberate in teaching those students to respect the dignity of all people. When teachers fail to effectively stop bullying, students believe that teachers must think it is OK. To a large extent, bullying persists because some teachers continue to tolerate it. **Olweus**, in his study, suggests that some bullying even comes from teachers who use rude sarcasm as a teaching tool.

There are teachers who are bullies and are allowed to use sarcasm, fear, intimidation and embarrassment as their classroom management strategy. If you, as the teacher, have ever embarrassed a student as an attempt to squelch inappropriate behavior, what are you teaching your students? Students know that if the teacher makes fun of a student, it is okay for them to make fun of that student, too. Students also know that they are not safe either. No matter how well they behave, your students know that some day you may embarrass them, too. Control based on fear is very destructive.

I want to make every educator reading this uncomfortable. If you abuse your power and are disrespectful to your students, no matter how lofty your goal, you are a **bully**. I have never found any value in calculatedly embarrassing students. Educators must put the "dunce-cap" mentality behind us. Yes, using fear, intimidation and sarcasm often works. Bullying can create a very orderly classroom or even country. Ask the Iraqi citizens who suffered under the rule of Saddam Hussein. A teacher who tries to prove that he is in control, in reality proves that he is not. If you can't tell the difference between classroom management and bullying, maybe you don't need to be teaching. Don't even try to address the issue of bullying among your students unless you are willing to examine your own personal beliefs, prejudices and behaviors first. What you do speaks so loudly! Your students' won't pay attention to what you say.

Review the handout *Are You an Educator, or Are You a Bully?* and look at yourself honestly. If you recognize any bullying behaviors, make a pledge to stop them now. Make apologies to your students if necessary, but make a commitment to be an "educator" and set the tone for your class by treating everyone in it with dignity and respect.

ARE YOU AN EDUCATOR, OR A BULLY?

Educators let students know they care.
Bullies let students know who's boss.

Educators teach self-control.
Bullies exert their own control.

Educators diffuse minor disruptions with humor.
Bullies use sarcasm to turn disruptions into confrontations.

Educators privately counsel those with chronic discipline problems.
Bullies publicly humiliate chronic misbehavers.

Educators help all students feel successful.
Bullies punish students for being unsuccessful.

Educators see each student's uniqueness.
Bullies compare children with one another.

Educators treat all students with respect.
Bullies make it clear that not all students deserve respect.

Educators highlight good behavior.
Bullies make examples of those with poor behavior.

Educators are aware of the power they wield and choose their words carefully.
Bullies wield their power recklessly, frequently resorting to anger and intimidation.

Educators educate.
Bullies humiliate.

Are you a bully?

Source: "Are You a Bully?" By Linda Starr (Education World.com, 02/04/2003.
Excerpted with permission

THE TEACHER AS THE MODEL

I have come to a frightening conclusion that I am the decisive element in the classroom... As a teacher; I possess tremendous power to make a child's life miserable or joyous. I can be a tool of torture or an instrument of inspiration. can humiliate or humor, hurt or heal. In all situations, it is my response that decides whether a crisis will be escalated or de-escalated, and a child humanized or dehumanized.

— Haim Ginott
Israeli Educator

I hope all of the teachers reading his quote know the correct choice in each of these paradigms. This quote helps us realize that the teacher has a tremendous impact on bullying in the classroom. The teacher's actions can serve to increase or decrease incidents of bullying.

- Take the time to build a trusting and caring relationship with all your students especially bullies and victims. Bullies rarely have a positive relationship with their teachers. Taking the time to build a trusting and caring relationship with a bully may be one of the most effective ways to end the bullying.

- Help every student become successful and valued for their own skills and talents. Students who have academic and social difficulties are often teased and intimidated by their peers.

- Model respect through your classroom management strategies. Teachers must maintain order in the classroom or teasing and bullying will flourish.

- Use discipline as an opportunity to teach the correct behavior. A teacher's discipline style has a big influence on bullying in the classroom. Remember that the word discipline is a form of the word disciple. If you will consider your students disciples, who are trying to follow your example, you may be more conscious of the way you respond to them.

- Use personal conferences with students to address chronic behavior problems. Public confrontations can give a bully the audience they want.

- Never engage in a power struggle with a student. I have heard that for every minute you argue with a child your age drops 5 years. It doesn't take long for you to be on their level and you are reinforcing their negative behavior.

- Create a safe classroom community. When students feel safe emotionally and physically, they are better able to concentrate on learning.

- Use cooperative groups, group learning and peer tutoring to build community in your classroom.

- Teach anger management and conflict resolution skills in your classroom.

- Use your curriculum to teach caring and moral and ethical behavior. Examine the subject(s) you teach and identify people and issues that can be discussed and explored while examining caring relationships and moral judgments.

TEACHER INTERVENTIONS FOR BULLIES

When teachers see bullying going on and do nothing to stop it, students may assume the teacher is condoning the bullying. Many times, the teacher is either unaware of what is happening or just not sure how to intervene appropriately. Examine the circumstances of the student interaction and decide on an intervention strategy that is appropriate for the student's behavior.

- Move closer to the students. Often your very presence will be enough to stop the bullying incident.

- When you see students exhibiting bullying behavior, stop the behavior immediately.

- Investigate to determine the seriousness of the situation and make an appropriate response. You do not want to over or under-react.

- Rather than accusing the bully of bullying, privately ask the bully questions.
  "What did you do?"
  "What was inappropriate about that?"
  "What is the rule that covers this behavior?"
  "Who did you hurt?"
  "What were you trying to accomplish?"
  "The next time that is your goal, how will you accomplish it without hurting another student?"
  "What are you going to do for the person you hurt?"

There are times when the victim may try to create the impression that he/she is not being bullied at all. The victim may prefer to suffer the indignity of being bullied rather than risk the greater embarrassment of having the teacher intervene on his/her behalf.

- Talk to the victim and/or bystanders separately and in private, at a later time to get a clearer picture of what is actually going on and how you can best help both the victim and bully.

- Make sure the bully and the victim get the support they need. Provide the victim with strategies she can use to prevent future bullying episodes or refer her to additional services. (Unit Five - *Skills for Bullies*, Unit six - *Skills for the Bullied*)

CONSEQUENCES AND STRATEGIES FOR ANGRY STUDENTS

1. Use "Time for Self" to allow a student a chance to cool down. Instruct the student to sit separately from the class and calm himself/herself down (Activity 5.1 *Time for Self.*) While the student is in "Time for Self," have him/her write a narrative of what happened. You may want to give the student these questions to write an answer to in relation to the incident.

   • Who was involved?
   • What did I do?
   • What did the other person do?
   • How did it make me feel?
   • How do you think the other person feels?
   • What could I have done differently?
   • What should my consequences be?

2. Have the angry student write or make an apology for his disrespectful comments or actions.

3. For every negative comment or action that took place during the incident, the student will make a positive comment or action.

4. The angry student will make restitution (repair or replace) any destroyed or damaged items.

5. The angry student may be assigned work around the school to make a positive contribution to the campus.

6. Help the angry student to identify illogical thoughts and learn to think differently (Activity 5.10 *Rational and Irrational Thoughts.*)

7. Use reverse role-playing to help the student develop empathy for the victim (Activity 5.13 *Who is the Bully Now?*)

8. Teach self-monitoring skills (Activity 5.3 *Self Monitoring.*)

9. Evaluate the needs of the student and provide skills training (Units Four, Five, Six and Seven.)

10. Help the student identify and develop his/her own interests.

11. Teach conflict resolution and anger management skills (Unit Two – *Consequences For Angry Students,* Activities 4.14 *We Have Different Ideas,* 4.15 *Conflicts Have Two Sides,* 4.16 *Mediation Works,* 6.10 *Relax,* & 6.11 *Relax and Move.*)

12. Provide opportunities for positive actions (Unit One – *Mix It Up At Lunch, Friendship Teams, Opportunities for Community Service.*)

STUDENT BEHAVIOR CONTRACTS

WHAT is a student behavior contract? Contracting is one technique that has been shown to be successful in increasing desirable or decreasing undesirable behaviors. A contract is a straightforward, unemotional, fair document that spells out plainly what is expected of the student and what the consequences are for breaking it. Contracting acknowledges a student's ability to control his/her behavior.

WHO should be given contracts? Contracting works best with students who are willing to acknowledge their inappropriate behavior and express a desire to improve. Contracting is especially appropriate with minor and/or first-time infractions of the discipline code. Students who have disorders (ADHD, Aspergers Syndrome, etc.) that often manifest themselves in inappropriate behavior (Unit Seven – *Helping the Victim with Special Needs*) should be given an opportunity to improve their behavior with contracts.

HOW should the contract be written? Contracts should be stated positively ("I want to learn") and not punitively ("because I have misbehaved"). The contract should focus on the behaviors you expect to see from the student. The goal of the contract should be to teach the student what to do and not just what not to do. Behaviors identified in the contract should be observable and measurable.

HOW will we know if it is successful? The contract must be evaluated for compliance. That means someone must follow up with the student and give him/her feedback on his/her progress. If a student needs to be monitored each period, send a copy of the contract to the teacher, with the form for the teacher to provide input. The student can be directed to bring the teacher evaluations to the person monitoring the contract at the end of the school day.

WHAT happens if the student fails to follow the contract? Clear feedback needs to be given to the student as to his/her success. If the student does not follow the contract, he/she has already agreed to consequences. Follow through with those consequences. Consequences should be logical for the student's behavior.

WHEN will the contract end? Inform the student when you feel you no longer need to monitor his/her behavior identified on the contract. Provide encouragement and praise for the student's successful following of the contract. I do not include "rewards" in my behavioral contracts. The good behavior itself and success should be rewarding enough for the student.

BEHAVIOR CONTRACT

Name _____

Date _____ Grade _____

Referring teacher _____

I realize that my behavior is causing problems for me. Because I want to learn and I realize it is unfair for me to _____

_____

_____

_____

I agree to _____

_____

_____

_____

My following this contract will be evaluated ☐ hourly ☐ daily ☐ weekly ☐ monthly, and I will be given feedback on my progress by _____ .

I understand that failing to abide by this agreement will result in the following consequence(s):

_____

_____

_____

_____

_____

Signature _____

Witness _____

TEACHER EVALUATION
OF CONTRACT COMPLIANCE

Name _____

Date _____ Grade _____

Teachers please review the Behavior Contract. In an effort to evaluate the success of this student, we need your input on his/her compliance. Please complete your evaluation and

❏ return the form to the student.

❏ return the form to the office.

Teacher _____ Period _____

Contract compliance: ❏ Good

                   ❏ Fair

                   ❏ Poor

Teacher _____ Period _____

Contract compliance: ❏ Good

                   ❏ Fair

                   ❏ Poor

Teacher _____ Period _____

Contract compliance: ❏ Good

                   ❏ Fair

                   ❏ Poor

Teacher _____ Period _____

Contract compliance: ❏ Good

                   ❏ Fair

                   ❏ Poor

Teacher _____ Period _____

Contract compliance: ❏ Good

                   ❏ Fair

                   ❏ Poor

Add any comments on the back. Thank you.

WHAT IS BULLYING?

Activity 2.1

Purpose
To help students better understand the definition of bullying.

Materials
Student handout – **What Is Bullying?**

Procedure
Tell the students that as we begin addressing the problem of bullying, we need to all be working with the same definition. Give the students the handout and ask them to complete it independently. Review the instructions and allow the students time to complete the handout.

Ask the class if they would be surprised to learn that all the answers on the handout are true. If some students disagree, discuss the response until they understand why the statement is true.

Divide the class into groups of 4 to 6 students. Instruct the students to use the information on their handout to develop a definition of bullying. Tell the students the amount of time they have to develop their definition (ten to fifteen minutes should be sufficient.)

Have each group share their definition with the class by making a poster, overhead or writing the definition on the chalk board. Encourage students to select the best definition or combine parts they like from several definitions. Use this definition to conduct other activities.

Post the definition of bullying in the classroom to refer to with other activities.

The class definition should be similar to this:
Bullying is a repeated, conscious, deliberate, hostile act intended to inflict pain, discomfort, embarrassment, and/or to induce fear through violence, the threat of violence or humiliation.

Follow-up
Ask the students:
- What makes bullying hard to define?
- Can any definition include the total impact bullying can have on an individual? Why/why not?
- What are some other true statements about bullying that we have not mentioned?

What Is Bullying?

Read each of the following statements and decide if the statement is true (T) or false (F). Record your answer in the blank

_____ Bullying is a conscious, willful act.

_____ Bullying is intended to inflict pain, discomfort, embarrassment and/or fear.

_____ Bullying is about the abuse of power.

_____ Bullies often like for others to think they are tough.

_____ Bullying can be in your face or behind your back.

_____ Bullying can be perpetrated by individuals, or a group.

_____ Bullies often make their attack without any real reason.

_____ Bullying can take many forms including gestures, extortion, exclusion and rumors.

_____ Making someone do something he/she doesn't want to do is also a form of bullying.

_____ Most bullying is done so that adults are not aware of it.

_____ Bullies may use prejudice related to race, gender, and/or religion to justify their bullying.

_____ Bullies often attack because they see their victim as an easy target.

_____ Bullying is the repetition of an unkind act.

_____ Bullies induce fear through violence, the threat of violence or humiliation.

_____ Bullies target victims because of their physical attributes or mental abilities.

STYLES OF BULLYING

Activity 2.2
"A" – Grades 5 & 6
"B" – Grades 7 - 12

Purpose
To help students identify the different styles of bullying.

Materials
Students handout – **Styles of Bullying "A" or "B"**
Chalk board, chart or overhead

Procedure
I have included two handouts for this activity. Handout "A" is more appropriate for younger students (grades 5 & 6.) Handout "B" deals with sexual harassment and gender identity issues as well as the other forms of bullying (grades 7 - 12.) Select the handout that is more appropriate for your students.

Explain to the students that bullying can take many forms. Identify that the four main styles of bullying are verbal, emotional, physical and harassment. If you are using handout "B" also identify sexual harassment as a particular type of harassment. Write these four categories on the chalkboard, dry erase board, chart or overhead. Ask students to identify the behaviors that should be listed under each. Use the information below to help student's categorize the different styles of bullying.

Verbal bullying is the most common form of bullying among both boys and girls. Verbal bullying can include teasing, name-calling, mocking, taunting and putdowns. Although gestures and dirty looks are a form of non-verbal communication, they are going to be included as a form of verbal bullying.

Emotional bullying may be more subtle than the other forms, but it is just as, if not more, painful for the victim. Emotional bullying can include isolation, rejection, ignoring, spreading rumors, manipulating others to cause rejection of someone and setting someone up for public embarrassment. Girls are more likely than boys to use emotional bullying against their victims.

Physical bullying includes hitting, kicking, pushing, slapping, spitting, tripping, choking, taking or defacing property and physical acts that demean and humiliate. This form of bullying is more common among boys.

Harassment is bullying that involves threats, extortion, coercion, challenging the person to do something they don't want to do and ethnic, racial, religious and sexual taunting.

Sexual Harassment is a specific form of harassment directed toward a person's sexual identity or behavior. Sexual harassment can be physical, verbal or emotional. It can include exhibitionism, voyeurism, propositions, suggestions, sexual gestures and spreading rumors. Girls are more emotionally distressed by this form of bullying than are boys. (See information on sexual harassment in the introduction of this book.)

STYLES OF BULLYING
Activity 2.2 *(continued)*

Give students the handout you have selected and go over the instructions. Have students complete the handout independently. After all students have completed the handout, go over the answers. Discuss any questions the students may have. It is not important that they all agree on the categories, but that they recognize the behavior as bullying.

Follow-up
Ask the Students:
- Were you aware that all these behaviors constituted bullying?
- What style of bullying do you observe the most at our school?
- Is all bullying in some way emotional?
- Does understanding the different styles of bullying help you be more conscious of your own bullying behaviors? How?

Additional questions for handout "B."
- Is sexual harassment more offensive than other forms of bullying?
- Does sexual harassment need to be addressed with different strategies than other forms of bullying?

Style of Bullying
"A"

Identify the style of bullying in each of the following statements as "V" for verbal, "E" for emotional, "P" for physical bullying and "H for harassment.

_____ 1. Calling someone names.

_____ 2. Taking someone's possessions.

_____ 3. Teasing people until they get upset.

_____ 4. Refusing to let someone join the group.

_____ 5. Hitting someone.

_____ 6. Spreading unkind rumors about someone.

_____ 7. Getting someone to do something that will be embarrassing.

_____ 8. Intentionally tripping someone.

_____ 9. Threatening someone to make them do something they don't want to do.

_____ 10. Making rude comments about the way someone dresses.

_____ 11. Challenging someone to do something to embarrass them.

_____ 12. Making a negative racial comment to someone.

_____ 13. Kicking someone.

_____ 14. Threatening someone to make them give you money.

_____ 15. Deliberately smearing catsup on someone.

_____ 16. Ignoring a person who is talking to you.

_____ 17. Beating someone up.

_____ 18. Encouraging others to leave a person out.

_____ 19. Teasing someone about their grades.

_____ 20. Pushing someone as a threat.

Style of Bullying "B"

Identify the style of bullying in each of the following statements as "V" for verbal, "E" for emotional, "P" for physical bullying and "H for harassment.

_____ 1. Calling someone names.

_____ 2. Taking someone's possessions.

_____ 3. Teasing people until they get upset.

_____ 4. Refusing to let someone join the group.

_____ 5. Hitting someone.

_____ 6. Spreading unkind rumors about someone.

_____ 7. Getting someone to do something that will be embarrassing.

_____ 8. Intentionally tripping someone.

_____ 9. Threatening someone to make them do something they don't want to do.

_____ 10. Calling someone gay or fag.

_____ 11. Making rude comments about the way someone dresses.

_____ 12. Challenging someone to do something to embarrass them.

_____ 13. Making a negative racial comment to someone.

_____ 14. Making comments concerning the size of a girl's breast.

_____ 15. Kicking someone.

_____ 16. Threatening someone to make them give you money.

_____ 17. Deliberately smearing catsup on someone.

_____ 18. Publicly suggesting someone commits certain sexual acts.

_____ 19. Ignoring a person who is talking to you.

_____ 20. Beating someone up.

_____ 21. Making gestures to someone that are sexual in nature.

_____ 22. Encouraging others to leave a person out.

_____ 23. Teasing someone about their grades.

_____ 24. Pushing someone as a threat.

_____ 25. Making negative comments concerning ethnic groups.

PLEDGES
Activity 2.3

Purpose
Students will make a commitment to model socially appropriate behavior.

Materials
Student handout **Nonviolent Pledge** or **No-Bullying Pledge** or poster paper with the pledge written on it.

Procedure
This procedure can be used with either the **Nonviolent** or **No Bullying Pledges**. Explain to the students that we are all concerned about acts of bullying/violence in our school. We all want to feel safe. While this pledge holds no magic solution to the problem of violence/bullying, it is a way of making a personal commitment to be part of the solution not part of the problem. Refusing to participate in violent/bullying behavior and making a commitment to report bullying/or potential danger we see is the best way for all of us to remain safe. While reporting can be hard and takes a lot of courage, it is the right thing to do for everyone.

Give everyone a copy of the **Nonviolent/No-Bullying Pledge** or display the poster with the pledge written on it. Encourage all students to sign the pledge, but do not make an issue if a student is reluctant to sign. I encourage all teachers to sign a copy of the pledge and post it where students can see.

Follow-Up
Ask the students:
- What makes it important to sign this pledge?
- If you did see bullying or something dangerous, who would you tell?
- Will you feel safer if all students sign this pledge?
- What would make you feel safer from bullying and other violence?

NONVIOLENCE PLEDGE

Because I want to feel safe from acts of violence at my school and I realize safety is everyone's responsibility,

I pledge to:

- Be a part of the solution even if others won't;

- Never bring any weapon to school;

- Not participate in any violent act or the planning of any violent act;

- Stay alert to any potential danger on our campus;

- Report any suspicions of danger to myself or others to the faculty or staff;

- Not encourage any student who is violent with my support or silence.

Name _____

Date _____

NO-BULLYING PLEDGE

Because I value the rights of others to learn and be treated with the respect they deserve, and because I do not like to be bullied and I realize that no one likes to be bullied, **I make the following pledge:**

- I will eliminate all bullying from my own behavior;

- I will refuse to join in when others are bullying, and I will encourage others to do the same;

- I will do my part to make this school a safe place to learn by being more sensitive to the feelings of others;

- I will treat everyone with respect;

- I will not use my words or actions to hurt others;

- I will intervene when I see someone being bullied if I can do so without making the situation worse;

- I will report the bullying incidents to an adult if I feel I cannot intervene.

Name _____

Date _____

BREAKING DOWN FEARS
Activity 2.4

Purpose
To help students learn the meaning of Dr. Kings quote.
To help students learn the importance of communication.

Materials
Student Handout – **Breaking Down Fears**

Procedure
Present the quote from Dr. King to the class and lead a discussion. You may use these questions to facilitate a discussion, but also encourage students to share their thoughts and feelings.
- What made Dr. King think that people didn't get along?
- What made Dr. King think people feared each other?
- What did Dr. King see as a solution to people not getting along?
- At the time that Dr. King made this statement, what groups of people were not getting along in the United States?
- What groups of people are not getting along in the world today?
  Could communication help these people get along better?
- What groups of people are not getting along in our school?
  Could communication help these people get along better?

Follow-up
Ask the students:
- Do you agree with Dr. King's quote? Why or Why not?
- What can you do to break down the fear between students in our school and improve communication?
- What is the main reason we are not able to communicate effectively with each other?

BREAKING DOWN FEARS

People don't get along because they fear each other.

People fear each other because they don't know each other.

They don't know each other because they have not properly communicated with each other.

**– Dr. Martin Luther King Jr.
Minister, Civil Rights Leader**

MEET MY NEW BEST FRIEND
Activity 2.5

Purpose
To help students get to know the other students in their class.

Materials
Student handout – **Meet My New Best Friend**

Procedure
This is a good first of the year or semester activity. This activity can be used with the whole class or with individual students.

Whole class - Have students pair with someone in the class whom they do not know very well. One way to create random pairs is to ask people with birthdays in January to stand. Begin to pair students based on the date of their birthdays moving from the first of the month to the end. If the students paired already know each other, skip to the next person. Continue through the year until everyone has been paired up.

Instruct the students to take turns interviewing their partner. You can use the interview questions on the student handout or create your own. The questions on the handout begin with less-sensitive information and progress to more personal and revealing information. Students will each have 10 minutes to find out as much as they can about their partner. After both students have had an opportunity to interview each other, bring the group back together. Be sure to tell students when it's time to begin and end their interviews.

After the interviews, have students take turns introducing their partner to the rest of the class. They are to begin their introduction – "Meet my new best friend, _____." Encourage the students to share things they learned in the interview without reading from the interview sheet.

Individual students – If you have students who aren't getting along but there is not open hostility, it can help to give them an opportunity get to know each other. Have them perform the interviewing assignment. They will then introduce each other to you. This activity can be a valuable tool for building mutual understanding, however it is important to know your students. Do not create an opportunity for a bully to abuse the information he/she may learn and make matters worse.

Follow-up
Ask the students:
- How has this activity helped you get to know each other?
- What are some of the things you found you have in common with others in the classroom?
- Did you learn some things about your classmates that surprised you?

MEET MY NEW BEST FRIEND

Your Name _____

Friend's Name _____

Interview another student and record their answers.

What is your favorite food? _____

What is your favorite TV show? _____

What is your favorite music group or singer? _____

What is your favorite movie? _____

What is your favorite sport? _____

What is the one possession that means the most to you? _____

What is the most important quality in a friend? _____

Who is the family member that means the most to you? _____

What is your dream career? _____

If you could go anywhere in the world, where would you go? _____

Who is the one person (living or dead) you would most like to meet?

_____

What is the place where you feel the happiest? _____

What is the biggest regret you have? _____

What is the one thing you would most like to accomplish?

_____

JUST LIKE ME

Activity 2.6

Purpose

To help students realize they have many things in common.

Materials

None

Procedure

Begin on one side of the room or call on the students in alphabetical order. Have each student stand and make a statement that is true about himself that other students in the class may not know. Examples: "I like baseball." "I have a horse." "I have had surgery." After the student makes his/her statement, any other student for whom that statement is also true will stand and say, "Just like me." Continue with each student until everyone has had a turn.

Follow-up

Ask the students:
- What did you learn about others in this room that you did not know?
- What do we have in common?
- Do we all have to be just alike to work together?
- How can differences enhance our ability to work together?

APPRECIATION TIME
Activity 2.7

Purpose
To give students an opportunity to share compliments with their classmates.

Materials
Paper cut into strips or, if desired, shapes like hearts, stars, flowers, etc.

Procedure
This activity needs to be used with a group or class that has already had an opportunity to get to know one another and has talked and shared openly. The activity can be used at the end of a semester or group project or it can be used on a regular (weekly, monthly, etc.) basis.

Tell the students that we are going to share compliments with our class members.

Option 1 – Prepare strips of paper (hearts, flowers, etc.) with each student's name written on one side. Randomly distribute the names throughout the class, giving each student one. Make sure no student has his/her own name. Instruct the students to write a compliment for the student whose name they were given on the other side of the paper. Starter statements could be:

> I really like the way you …
> You are really good at …
> Something really special about you is …

Give the compliment back to the person for whom it was written.

Option 2 – Give every student several strips of paper, one for each student in the room. Instruct the students to write a compliment for each student in the room or group, printing the name of the recipient on the back of each slip of paper. You can use the above prompts. Give the compliments to the person for whom it was written.

Follow-up
Ask the students:
- Was it hard to think of a compliment? Why or Why not?
- How did it feel to get a compliment(s) from your peers?
- Why do you think we don't give each other compliments more often?
- How would your life be different if you got complimented every day?
- Will you make a commitment to give someone else a compliment today?

CLASS RULES ABOUT BULLYING

Activity 2.8

Purpose
To have student's participate in rule development.
To have students make clear rules against bullying.

Materials
Chalk board, chart or overhead

Procedure
Tell the students that it is important that the classroom be a safe place for everyone to learn. That means bullying and disrespect will not be allowed. Today, we are going to set down some rules regarding bullying so everyone is clear about how we will treat one another.

Pose the following question to the class.
What kind of classroom do we want? Begin to make a list of statements from the students on the board or chart. After you have a good list on the board,

Pose this second question.
How can we make this happen? If this is where we want to go, how can we get there? What rules do we need in order to have the kind of class we want?

Chose one of the following activities to continue.

Rule Development Activity I
- Have the students suggest possible rules that would benefit the class. All suggestions are recorded on the board.
- Hold a class discussion on each rule. Discuss the purpose of the rule and have students give specific examples of incidents in which the rule would be broken. The class will eliminate some suggestions.
- Once the list has been narrowed down encourage the class to look at the list and see if there are items that can be combined.
- Continue reworking and combining the suggestions until you have no more than six to eight rules for the class.

Rule Development Activity II
- Have each student write down at least three things he/she thinks should be included in the anti-bullying rules.
- Have the students form pairs or small groups. Each member is to share his/her suggested rules with his/her group. After everyone in the group has shared, they will use everyone's suggestions to produce a set of four rules to present to the class.

- Have each group report its suggestions to the class. List the rules on the board. The group members should report their reasons for suggesting the rules they did.
- Have the students group the suggestions that are similar.
- The teacher can then take the suggestions from the class and come back the next day with a set of rules that would cover everything the students have discussed.

Publicize and Practice Rules

PUBLICIZE
Post the rules clearly in the room. Send a copy of the rules home to the parents. You may want to have the parents sign a statement saying they have read and understand the rules.

EXPLAIN
Discuss specific expectations for each rule and give examples. Model and have students' role-play proper behavior.

RE-TEACH
Re-teaching the rules will be necessary at certain times throughout the year - especially after a long break or holiday. Re-teaching the rules when a new student joins the class is also an effective way to remind the students of their rules and why they were chosen.

Follow-up
Ask the students:
- Since we all made the rules, how can we help each other keep the rules?
- What will you like best about a bully-free classroom?
- What can we do if we see someone being bullied?

89

BOOKS ABOUT BULLYING

Teachers can use books about bullying as a way for helping students understand the impact of bullying on others and a way to use open discussions concerning bullying. Select books that are appropriate for your age level.

Fiction Books About Bullying

Blume, Judy – *Blubber*

Casely, Judith – *The Bully*

DePino, Catherine – *Blue Cheese Breath and Stinky Feet*

Estes, Elinor – *The Hundred Dresses*

Filitti, J. & Erbes, E – *Out of This World – Tiglos vs. Secca Ma*

Flake, Sharon – *The Skin I'm In*

Golding, William - *Lord of the Flies*

Hahn, Mary Downing – *Stepping On The Cracks*

Hughes, Thomas - *Tom Brown's School Days*

Kinsey-Warnock, Natalie – *The Night The Bells Rang*

McCain, Becky Ray – *Nobody Knew What to Do*

Miko, Imou – *Lily's Secret*

O'Neill, A & Huliska, Beith – *The Recess Queen*

Peretti, Frank – *Hangman's Curse*

Seskin, S & Shamblin, A. – *Don't Laugh At Me*

Shreve, Susan – *Joshua T. Bates In Trouble Again*

Zindel, Paul – *Attack of the Killer Fishsticks*

Non-Fiction Books About Bulling

Blanco, Jodee – *Please Stop Laughing at Me*

Pelzer, Dave – *The Privilege of Youth*

Peretti, Frank - *The Wounded Spirit*

Wiseman, Rosalind – *Queen Bees and Wannabes*

Unit Three
Families Make a Difference – Skills for Parents

FAMILIES MAKE A DIFFERENCE: SKILLS FOR PARENTS

The most important thing in my child's education, in fact his/her entire life, is the attitude toward school and toward life that he/she leaves home with each morning.

— P. Lynch Whatley
Chairman, Lee County Board of Education

FAMILIES MAKE A DIFFERENCE

When families and educators work together, schools get better and students get a higher quality educational experience. Schools must realize that parents hold a critical roll in developing their children's behavioral and learning habits. Educators must assume that all parents want their children to be academically successful and well behaved and they often need our guidance on how to be most effective.

Many parents are able to prepare their children well for school, but there are many others who want to help their children but do not come to school. This fact should not be taken as evidence that they do not care. We must realize that job and family demands leave little free time for many parents. Their children are more often at risk of having academic and behavioral problems. Educational surveys show that most parents, regardless of their background, want guidance from the school on ways to help their children.

Students feel parent involvement will make them safer. A 2001 report from the *Horatio Alger Association* tells us that 27% of teens felt that a lack of parental involvement was the biggest cause of school violence. A 2001 study by the *Violence Policy Center* investigated thirty-seven violent incidents in schools. They found that guns were by-far the weapon of choice and that in nearly two-thirds of the incidents the student attackers obtained the guns from their own home or the home of a relative. Parents can directly impact a student's access to guns and need to be reminded of their responsibility regarding firearms.

Communication between the parents and the school often needs to be improved. Parents should be kept informed about anti-bullying efforts. Parents should be encouraged to contact the school when they have concerns. According to the *Gallup News Service* survey (2001), 32% of parents fear for their child's physical safety when the child is at school. 39% of parents with a child in grade six or higher are more likely to say they fear for their child's safety. 22% of parents whose children are in grade five or lower fear for their child's safety. Parent involvement in an anti-bullying program can help alleviate these fears. Research indicates that good relationships with parents, teachers or friends tended to shield young people from violence. Students with positive, supportive relationships are less likely to be victims or bullies.

Family practices in early childhood are clearly associated with later antisocial and delinquent behaviors. Educators must be more deliberate in breaking down the barriers that discourage parents from becoming more involved in the school. Schools must change their focus and realize that parents involvement really means sharing the responsibility of educating and disciplining the student with the parents. Schools and homes that lovingly set clear limits and boundaries and are nurturing and caring can probably prevent bullying. Parent involvement really eases the school's burden and can provide teachers more time for educating.

I know that not all parents are willing to work with the school. I have experienced my share of conferences with the "Parent from Hell." Not all parents will buy into the school's stand on bullying or the nonviolence approach of dealing with conflict. I have listened to numerous students justify their behavior with "My mama told me that if someone hit me, I had to hit them back." In too many families violence is considered a solution and no one listens to each other unless they are angry. These are the students that need our help the most and are the most at-risk. While the school can not get all parents on their side, it must get as many as it can on board for an anti-bullying program. If you can't find support for nonviolence outside the school, you can still create a safe caring environment within the school and you must try.

STRATEGIES TO HELP PARENTS

1. **Providing school support for family life.**
   - Make parents feel welcome in the school.
   - Host school-sponsored family activities.
   - Provide academic opportunities at the school for parents. The school can offer English as a second language classes, a G.E.D. program, computer classes, etc.
   - Conduct workshops that teach parents how to help their children improve academically in school.
   - Hold parenting classes to help parents provide appropriate, non-violent discipline.
   - Provide opportunities for parents to volunteer in the school. Let parents know that their help is needed and valued.

2. **Include parents in the development and implementation of the anti-bullying program and related discipline policies.**
   - Invite leaders in your parent association to participate and/or identify other parents who need to be involved. Make sure your parent representatives fairly represent the diversity in your school.
   - Communicate anti-bullying plans and policies to all parents (Unit one – *Planning a School Wide Anti-Bullying Campaign & Anti-Bullying Policy*, Unit Three - *Communication With Parents & Parent Pledge*.)

3. **Educate parents concerning bullying.**
   - Provide opportunities for parents to participate in school based training concerning bullying. Provide information on bullying, its impact and how parents can help. (Introduction, Unit one – *Bullying and Violence, Bullying and Learning*, Activities 2.1 *What is Bullying & 2.2 Style of Bullying*, Unit three – *Characteristics of Families that Bully, Characteristics of Families of Victims, How Do I Know If My Child is Being Bullied?, What Can I Do If My Child is Being Bullied?, How Do I Know If My Child Is Bullying Others?, What Can I Do If My Child is a Bully?*) Share information from the school based bullying survey found in Unit One with the parents.
   - Provide information concerning the impact of bullying and how parents can assist the school in helping parents who are not able to come to the school. (Introduction - *Why Deal With Bullying*, Unit Six – *Help the Victim*.)
   - Have parents complete the *School Bullying Survey – For Parents and Teachers* in Unit One and Activity 1.2 – *School Safety Survey* and provide parents with feedback.

4. **Provide parents with information concerning bullying that they can utilize at home.**
   - Provide parents with skills training activities from Unit Four if their child has been bullying other students.
   - If their child has special needs, provide assistance with skills training for identified deficits found in Unit Seven.
   - Provide parents with skills training activities from Unit Six if their child is being bullied.

COMMUNICATION WITH PARENTS

The school is in the unique position of coordinating communication and contact with parents. Parents look to the school for support and guidance with issues such as bullying. I have included handouts that can be used or adapted for use with your parents. Schools must remember that parent support is critical to the success of an anti-bullying program. Do your best to keep parents informed and provide support to your parents.

Parents are an essential link in the success of an anti-bullying program. A 2001 article in *Time* reported that the success of an anti-bullying program is 60% grounded in whether the same kinds of approaches are used at home. This means it is essential for schools to involve parents in every component of the planning and implementing of an anti-bullying program.

Parents need to be educated concerning the negative impact of bullying and provided with parenting strategies to use with their children at home. Schools need to conduct meetings with parents and disseminate information to parents to make them aware of the school's anti-bullying plan of action. Educators must be creative in devising new ways to make information accessible to parents. If students are not diligent in getting information to their parents, schools can use the mail or e-mail information to parents. Schools can use websites to post important policies and provide information to parents. Information provided by the school can improve the home environment and have a positive influence on the school environment.

I have included a parent letter that can accompany information on bullying, bullying policies and/or parenting information.

95

Dear Parent/Caregiver,

Most of us remember times from our school days when students were bullied. Bullying is not a new problem but it has been getting more attention recently. We have become more aware of the devastating impact that bullying can have on the victim, the bully and the entire school climate.

We want all our parents to join with the school in having a new attitude toward bullying. What used to be accepted as "kids will be kids" must change. We know that bullying is not just a "right of passage" but bullying is serious. Bullies often grow up to be abusive adults and young victims can suffer serious emotional problems in many areas of their lives. When students witness bullying, they are distracted, intimidated and can become emotionally upset. Bulling in schools prevents students from feeling safe, from learning and interferes with teachers teaching.

The school is making a serious commitment to do something about bullying. All the teachers, administrators and staff members of the school are sincere about their desire to make a difference.

The school is developing policies specifically concerning bullying. We will be conducting several programs throughout the year concerning bullying and we will make every effort to keep you informed. We will be sending home materials to keep you informed and provide helpful information. Please let us know how you would like to receive this information. If you ever have question or concerns, please contact the school.

Sincerely,

Parent(s) Name _____

Child(ren's) Name(s) _____

☐ Send materials with my child.

☐ Use e-mail, my address is _____

☐ Please mail the information to my home/work. The address is:

_____

_____

PARENT PLEDGE

The school can assist parents who want to join and support each other in protecting their children. It would probably be appropriate to have your parent teacher association sponsor this program and the school help facilitate the distribution and collection of the forms.

Parents have to be more concerned than ever with whom their child is associating with, where they are going and what happens in other peoples homes. Having parents sign a pledge and agree to be contacted by other parents, can assist parents in making a better decision concerning their child's activities. Signing a pledge will not guarantee that a parent will appropriately supervise activities but it does show an agreement with supervision and an intent to supervise appropriately.

I have included a sample parent pledge. This can be adapted for your school and your special needs. You will probably want to include a disclaimer of liability for your school and parent organization. A list of parents who sign the pledge will be distributed to all parents. Parents will then be better able to make good decisions concerning whom their children can visit and/or attend parties in the homes of others. Hopefully, this will create increased communication and support between parents who want to keep their children safe.

PARENT PLEDGE
KEEP OUR KIDS SAFE

To help in creating a safe and violence free environment for our children, I (we) pledge:

1. **I will teach my child to respect all people and to settle his/her conflicts nonviolently;**

2. **I will instruct my child that bullying is not acceptable;**

3. **I will supervise my child and all children who visit in my home and monitor their TV, video and Internet use;**

4. **I will be present at all parties held in my home and provide appropriate supervision;**

5. **Alcohol and other drugs will not be available or allowed to be consumed, with my knowledge, by children or youth in my home;**

6. **I welcome telephone calls about my child and about activities/parties in my home;**

7. **I agree to have my name and the information listed below published as a subscriber to this pledge.**

Parent(s) Name(s)	Home Phone	Work Phone

Child(ren)'s Names	Grade

PROACTIVE STRATEGIES
THAT CAN PREVENT BULLYING

Families that are nurturing and caring and set clear limits can prevent bullying as well as victimization. If you want to prevent your child from becoming a bully or a victim:

- Teach your child to be both strong and kind;

- Encourage your child to be a good friend because good friends don't bully;

- Only use nonphysical discipline to correct inappropriate behavior;

- Monitor the whereabouts of your child;

- Know your child's friends and make sure everyone understands your view of teasing and violence;

- Set a good example by exercising appropriate conflict resolution;

- Make sure your child understands that there are consequences for aggressive behavior;

- Teach your child not to hit or fight back; it often only makes things worse;

- Allow your child to feel what they feel but help them find ways to express their angry feelings without hurting others;

- Listen to your child's concerns. Let him/her know that you have time for what ever concerns them;

- Talk with your child about computer ethics, and establish rules of conduct and consequences for misuse of the Internet and/or e-mail;

- Instruct your child to never share his/her passwords or get into an argument with someone online;

- Monitor your child's television, video, and Internet viewing and make sure it is appropriate;

- Set rules for instant messaging (IM) and monitor your child's use of chat rooms;

- If you have firearms in your home make sure they are secured!

CHARACTERISTICS OF FAMILIES THAT BULLY

Family practices in early childhood are clearly associated with later antisocial and delinquent behaviors. While many bullying behaviors are learned in the home, schools must remember that not all bullies are the product of violent or neglectful homes.

- The home lives of bullies often lack nurturing and include neglect, rejection, emotional coldness and little affection.

- The parents of bullies are more likely to use abusive physical punishment inconsistently in their discipline.

- Bullies often experience a greater likelihood of a chaotic home environment. There are frequent parent conflicts, divorces, parents and stepparents coming in and leaving the home repeatedly and moves are common.

- The families of bullies are more likely to be socially isolated. There is a conscious effort to cut the family off from friends and extended family visitations. The parents teach their children to distrust people outside their family.

- Child-rearing practices in the home are randomly administered and usually ineffective. Children never know from one day to the next what will be acceptable and what will be punished.

- There is usually a lack of monitoring of the TV, movies, Internet, friends, music, videos and grades.

- Families seldom use problem solving strategies and violence is considered a solution.

- Families of bullies often have substance abuse issues and the children see and have access to inappropriate activities.

CHARACTERISTICS OF FAMILIES OF VICTIMS

Being a victim of bullying may also indicate that there are problems in the family dynamics.

- There may be sibling abuse or abuse by the parents in the home. Victims at home are more likely to be victims at school.

- The families of victims often have financial and/or marital problems. Children feel insecure and often don't have the clothing and "stuff" that the other students have.

- The families of victims may be overly emotionally involved and entangled in their children's difficulties. Parents consistently rescue their child and the child then fails to develop appropriate problem solving skills.

- The families of victims may become deeply involved in responding to the child's troubles. The more suffering the child experiences, the more the child depends on his/her parents to "save" him/her.

- The child's identity becomes that of a victim and the parents chronic rescuing reinforces this identity. There is often over-dependence by the victim on the parents for support.

- The parents may also have deficits in their social skills and therefore unable to help their children learn appropriate social skills.

SIBLING ABUSE

Sibling abuse is the more common than spousal or parent-child abuse. With more and more blended families and more children left in the care of siblings this abuse is on the rise. It occurs when sibling interactions become violent and the sibling feels powerless to stop the interaction. If one sibling is consistently singled out, abuse is occurring.

- Allow your child to have negative feelings toward his/her sibling(s). Encourage him/her to talk about these feelings.

- Help your child express his/her feeling in appropriate ways and explain how he/she would like to be treated.

- Help your child express his/her negative feelings into a creative outlet. Have him/her write a letter or draw a picture expressing his/her feeling.

- Encourage physical activities to expel angry feelings. Help your child learn to calm down after a conflict and relax.

- Always intervene and stop hurtful behavior but require the children to practice problem solving.

- Never make comparisons between children and avoid labeling your children. Express what you like about each child without comparing.

- Make it clear to all your children that you expect them to settle conflict without violence.

- Some squabbling needs to be ignored but intervene when one of the children becomes unhappy with the behavior.

- When you intervene in your children's disputes, model problem solving skills. Ask the following questions and take your children through this process:
  - What is the problem?
  - What are some possible solutions?
  - Which solution are you going to choose?

Check with the children later and ask:
How is the solution working?

HOW DO I KNOW IF MY CHILD IS BEING BULLIED?

Amazingly, parents frequently don't realize when their child is being victimized. Children are embarrassed and are afraid you will be ashamed of them for being teased. As the parent, you must learn to look for the subtle messages that show their child is having problems.

Your children may be a victim of bullying if they:

- Begin to act moody, sullen, or withdraw from interactions;

- Become depressed for no obvious reason;

- Loses interest in school and refuses to go;

- Start having their grades drop;

- Withdraws from school activities;

- Begin to have a loss of appetite or problems sleeping;

- Waits to use the restroom until they get home from school;

- Are unusually hungry after school;

- Become sad, sullen, angry or scared after receiving a phone call or email.

- Have torn or missing clothes;

- Have unexplained bruises or injuries;

- Stop talking about peers or asking to participate in activities with peers;

- Use insulting or demeaning language when talking about peers;

- Begins to complain of stomachaches, headaches, or have panic attacks;

- Begins having difficulty sleeping or sleeps too much and are still exhausted.

- Begins to need extra money for school lunch or supplies.

WHAT CAN I DO IF MY CHILD IS BEING BULLIED?

If you are concerned that your child is being bullied:

- Ask your child directly if he/she is being bullied. Many times he/she won't put forward the information due to the shame and embarrassment or due to fear;

- Believe your child, listen without interrupting and gather as many facts as you can including how your child responded to the bully;

- Don't promise to keep the bullying a secret. Explain that reporting the bully is the best way to get help;

- Don't blame your child and assure him/her that being bullied is not his/her fault. Don't minimize, justify or explain away the bully's behavior;

- Talk to your child about handling the situation. Don't rush in to solve the problem for your child. Ask if he/she needs help. If he/she says "No," follow up and ask again later;

- Become familiar with the school's policy on bullying and follow the described procedure for reporting the bullying;

- Don't encourage your child to fight back;

- Keep records of dates, times, places, names of those involved and the names of witnesses. Be able to describe the impact the bullying has had on your child as well as what your child has done to try to stop the bullying;

- Encourage your child to report the incident to school officials. Identify a school staff member your child feels comfortable talking to. Practice with your child how to make the report;

- Don't blame the school but work with your school to make sure your child is safe and the school is monitoring the situation;

- Be patient with the school. They will need time to investigate and develop a plan;

- Inform the school if you feel the problem is not being adequately addressed by the school. Express your concern to the teacher and/or administrator and if necessary, to the school district board office. If there is serious abuse, racism or sexual bullying you may make a report to the police.

Help your child develop skills to deal with bullying more effectively.

- Find positive activities that will help your child's self-esteem. Try to arrange involvement in positive social groups that interest your child especially if your child is timid and lacks friends.

- Enroll your child in a good martial arts program. When your child knows that he/she can take care of himself/herself, he/she will look and feel more assertive and will be less likely to be a victim.

- Make sure your child knows how to be safe and who to go to for help at school.

- Honestly reflect on your child's behavior. Is he/she doing something that might be encouraging the bully to pick on him/her?

- If your child has special needs, help him/her deal with deficits that may exist and provide skills training in areas of social deficits.

- Acknowledge your child's feelings and take them seriously

- Help your child find a safe route to and from school. Point out places where your child can go for help. Encourage your child to travel with friends.

- Encourage your child to speak to the bully in a calm and clear voice, name the behavior he/she doesn't like and state what is expected instead.

- Ask the school for help in providing skills to use with the bully. Practice with your child and find a style that fits with your child's personality.

- If necessary, seek counseling for your child to deal with the trauma of being bullied.

If your child is being bullied, don't:

- Ignore or minimize your child's complaints. Your child could be seriously hurt emotionally or physically;

- Tell your child to just ignore the bully. Bullies rarely just go away and your child needs to learn how to deal with them;

- Advise your child to hit back. Aggression among children can escalate quickly and too many children carry weapons.

HOW DO I KNOW IF MY CHILD IS BULLYING OTHERS?

Children can develop bullying behaviors as early as preschool and it can often go unnoticed by adults. It may not be your fault your child is bullying but it can be your fault if your child continues to bully.

Your child may be bullying others if they:

- Seem to enjoy having power, control and dominating others;

- Are physically larger or older than their peers;

- Seem to enjoy seeing others experience fear, embarrassment, or pain;

- Show little or no empathy or compassion for the feelings of others;

- Justify his/her violent behaviors and blame the victim reporting that they "deserved it;"

- Demonstrates little remorse of his/her negative behaviors;

- Seem more concerned with their needs and desires, without regard for the needs of others;

- Have friends who do whatever he/she says;

- Have more money or other possessions than they should have with vague explanations as to where the items came from;

- Are unable to see things from the other person's point of view;

- Seem to enjoy conflict and/or fights;

- Idolize people who are violent, aggressive or powerful;

- Spend excessive amounts of time watching violent movies or playing violent video games;

- Spend excessive amounts of time on the Internet or in questionable chat-rooms;

- Is disrespectful of rules and authority. Feels that the rules don't apply to him/her.

WHAT CAN I DO IF MY CHILD IS A BULLY?

Not all bullies are the product of a violent or neglectful home. Even if your child is good and popular, they may still be disrespectful with their peers. If your child is bullying others, he/she is also experiencing psychological harm.

- No parent wants to admit that their child is a bully. Be careful not to become defensive.

- Do not make excuses, try to "wait out" or ignore the problem. Most bullies do not out grow their aggressiveness.

- Find out as much as you can about the problem.

- Make it clear to your child that you will not tolerate bullying behavior.

- Determine if your child is a leader or just one of the followers.

- If your child is a follower, keep him/her away from the leader and perhaps even the entire group.

- Supervise your child more closely and monitor his/her friends.

- If your child is the leader, cooperate with the teachers and other parents in monitoring your child's activities.

- Be aware that patterns of aggression and intimidation can become ingrained. The longer the bullying behaviors persist, the more difficult the behaviors are to change.

- Expect your child to acknowledge responsibility for his/her behavior and accept the consequences that are given.

- Help your child be able to make a sincere apology to his/her victim and make meaningful reparations.

- Administer an effective, non-violent consequence that is age appropriate and fits the offense.

- Avoid the temptation to personally pay for damages or injury. Insist your child make restitution; offer his/her personal property for restitution or work to pay for damages.

- Ask the school and other parents to report back to you if your child resumes any form of bullying or intimidation.

- Forbid your child from watching violence on TV, videos or movies. Limit all use of violence based video games (usually marked with a "M" rating.)

- Work with your child on developing empathy for his/her victim and discuss the personal impact that bullying can have.

- Examine your family communication. Bullying can frequently be triggered by anxiety in the child caused by problems with a care-giver, a new baby in the house or a change in school.

- Work to improve family communication. Plan more family dinners and activities.

- If necessary, seek counseling to understand why he/she felt the need to intimidate and bully others.

PARENT RESOURCES

Blue Cheese Breath and Stinky Feet by Catherine DePino

Bullies Are a Pain In the Brain by Trevor Romain

Bullies and Victims: Helping Your Child Through the Schoolyard Battle by SuEllen and Paula Fried

Don't Laugh At Me by Seskin & Shamblin

Eliminating Bullying By Sandy Ragona & Kerri Pentel

Enemy Pie: A Tale About Handling Relationships and Conflict by Derek Munson

Getting Equipped to Stop Bullying by Boatwright, Mathis & Smith-Res

Girl Wars: 12 Strategies That Will End Female Bullying by Dellasega & Nixon

How to Handle Bullies, Teasers and Other Meanies by Kate Cohen-posey

How to Raise Kids With Solid Character, Strong Minds, and Caring Hearts by Michele Borba

How to Talk So Kids Can Learn At Home and in School by Adele Faber & Elaine Mazlish

Making and Keeping Friends by John Schmidt

Mean Chicks, Cliques and Dirty Tricks by Erida Shearin-Karres

Nah! Nah! Nah! by Richard Diren

No More Bullies! by Marcia Shoshana-Nass

Nobody Knew What To Do by Becky Ray McCain

Parents Do Make a Difference by Michele Borba

Positive Discipline A-Z: 1001 Solutions to Everyday Parenting Problems by Nelson, Lott & Glenn

200 Ways to Raise a Boy's Emotional Intelligence by Will Glennon

200 Ways to Raise a Girl's Self-Esteem by Will Glennon

Teaching Your Children Sensitivity by Linda & Richard Eyer

The Girls and Boys Book About Good and Bad Behavior by Richard Gardner

Your Child's Emotional Health: The Middle Years by Philadelphia Child Guidance Center w/ Jack Maguire

Unit Four
Empowering the Bystander –
Skills for Students

EMPOWERING THE BYSTANDERS: SKILLS FOR STUDENTS

I AM ONLY ONE,

BUT STILL I AM ONE.

I CANNOT DO EVERYTHING,

BUT I CAN DO SOMETHING;

AND BECAUSE I CANNOT DO EVERYTHING

I WILL NOT REFUSE TO DO THE

SOMETHING THAT I CAN DO

— Edward Everett Hale (1822-1909)
American Author and Clergyman

Unit Four
EMPOWERING THE BYSTANDERS: SKILLS FOR STUDENTS

Bullying will stop when students decide it will stop. The 2000 *National Institute of Child Health and Human Development* survey found that 17% of the respondents had been bullied recently, 19% had bullied others recently and 6% had both bullied others and been bullied. We can conclude that most students are not chronically bullying their peers or being bullied by their peers but most are witnessing these daily attacks. The show can't go on without an audience. When this "silent majority" feels empowered and possesses skills to speak up and intervene appropriately, bullies will lose their power. When all students are empowered to stand up against injustices, encouraged to act with integrity, taught to resist provocation, and learn to resolve conflicts peacefully, bullying will no longer be a problem. You will outnumber the bullies if you teach the "silent majority" to stand up and act.

In some cases of bullying, others are standing by feeling helpless, afraid to speak up. Students see the victim of bullying being rejected by peers and they think, "That could be me," If students aren't taught otherwise, they may side with the bully because they don't know what else to do. They stand idly by and through acts of omission become the supporting cast who actually aid and abet the bully. Even "nice students" who know better may be frightened that the bully may turn on them. Bystanders must realize that they have the power to escalate the violence by providing support and encouragement to the bully or to become peacemakers if they choose to act with bravery and integrity. When bullies are confronted with a united gathering of their peers who support the victim and believe that bullying is not acceptable, the bully's power is neutralized. Peers must communicate to the bullies that they will not be looked up to, nor will their cruel behavior be condoned or tolerated. An anti-bullying program is incomplete unless it includes strategies to empower all students with self-confidence and skills in conflict resolution, anger management and empathy.

Few failed to see the 2003 videotape of the students at Glenbrook North High School in Northbrook, Illinois. As a crowd of students watched, seniors girls kicked punched and slapped junior girls in a brutal rites of passage. Buckets of paint, fish guts and other foul substances were thrown at the younger girls. Five of the girls had to be hospitalized. What made this video even more offensive were the comments of the crowd egging the offenders on. These disgusting actions could not have continued without the support of the bystanders. The crowd taunted as girls begged for assistance. Teens may be becoming desensitized to sheer grossness by viewing television programs such as: Fear Factor, Survivor or any of the other reality shows that abuse, humiliate, and exploit their contestants. We must raise questions about American culture and the role the media plays in it.

There are times when the bystanders lack compassion for the victim of bullying. As students get older, they report feeling less empathy for the victim. In their minds students rationalize that bad things don't just keep happening to good people, so the victim must be doing something wrong. Students reason that if bullying is so wrong, why doesn't someone stop it? They may conclude that if a person continues to be a victim then he/she must be doing something to deserve the abuse. Bystanders are negatively affected when bullying occurs and there appear to be no consequences for the bully. Blaming the victim is a common reaction among students and adults. Schools can no longer imply through non-action that the victim is at fault.

EMPOWERING THE BYSTANDERS: SKILLS FOR STUDENTS (continued)

Studies in England and Australia showed that while most students were opposed to bullying and felt supportive of the victim, only half tried to help the victims, and another one-third regretted not helping. *The National Center for Education Statistics, 1998 Bureau of Justice Statistics* reported:

- 56% of students report witnessing some type of bullying at school.

- 71% of students report incidence of bullying as a problem at their school.

- 43% of students report they try to help the victim, and 33% said they should help but do not.

You can't ask students to tell a bully to leave someone alone unless the school staff is willing to take action too. When students feel that the school staff is serious about addressing the issue of bullying, when they feel confident in their intervention skills, and know they will be supported by the staff, they are more likely to act responsibly and defuse conflict among their classmates. You can't ask students to tell a bully to leave someone alone unless the principal and staff have shown the courage to take action, too.

KOHLBERG'S STAGES OF MORAL DEVELOPMENT

The school should not expect students to make moral decisions that exceed their level of maturation. Lawrence Kohlberg identified the development of moral decision making. He pointed out that the Stages of Moral Development is linier and all humans must move through this process in the same order. Unfortunately, some individuals never reach the highest level of moral development. The school must help students realize that certain behaviors are wrong and encourage students to feel an obligation to do what is right. Everyone knows that stealing is wrong, but that doesn't stop certain people from doing it. Just because a child has been taught that fighting is wrong and against the rules, it does not follow that he/she will never fight unless he/she feels an obligation to do what is right.

The **Pre-conventional** stage of moral development usually continues until a child is about 10 or 11 years of age. At this level, there is no internalization or moral reasoning. Children obey because adults tell them to. Moral thinking is based on rewards and self interest.

In the **Conventional reasoning** stage, the person abides by the standards of others (parents, the law or society) but seldom stops to examine the accuracy of those standards. This stage usually lasts until late adolescents and even into early adulthood. Children often adopt their parents' moral standards, wanting to be a "good girl" or "good boy."

At these two stages of moral development, the child is extremely dependant on the adults in his/her life to form moral beliefs. This is why it is critical for the administration, staff and parents to support the same moral values of non-violence and respect for the individual. If the moral values at home are not reflective of our basic cultural values, it is even more critical that the adults in the school model and support kindness and caring.

In the **Post-conventional reasoning** stage morality is completely internalized and the person understands that values and laws are relative and that standards may vary from one person to another. He/she knows that laws are important but that laws can and, at times, should be changed. He/she believes that some values, such as liberty, are more important than the law.

The person has developed a moral standard based on universal human rights. When faced with a conflict between law and conscience the person will follow conscience even though the decision might involve personal risk.

STRATEGIES TO EMPOWER THE BYSTANDER

All students need to learn to be responsible, resourceful, compassionate human beings, who can stand up for themselves, and exercise their own rights while respecting the rights and needs of others.

1. Present the students with education on bullying and its consequences. (Introduction, Activities 2.1 *What Is Bullying?*, 2.2 *Styles of Bullying*, 4.1 *Lets Discuss Bullying*, 4.2 *Bullying is About Power*, 4.3 *Write About Bullying* & 4.4 *Read About Bullying*.)

2. Help students build friendship skills and bonds within the classroom. (Unit One – *Mix It Up At Lunch, Friendship Teams, Opportunities for Community Service*, Unit Two – *The Teacher as the Model*, Activities 2.4 *Breaking Down Fears*, 2.5 *Meet My New Best Friend*, 2.6 *Just Like Me*, 2.7 *Appreciation Time*, 4.13 *Lets Be Friends*, 5.14 *I can Help*, 5.15 *Let's Be Kind*, 6.12 *Enemies or Friends*, 6.13 *Making Friends* & 6.14 *Treating Others With Respect*.)

3. Train students in assertiveness and intervention skills. Students do not need to stand helplessly by and witness bullying behaviors nor do they need to try to bully the bully. The inappropriate intervention can escalate the situation and make matters much worse.

   - Teach students to assess the risk to themselves and others. (Activities 4.5 *Should I Help?*, 6.4 *Think Safety First* & 6.5 *Be Safe Going To and From School*)
   - Help students learn to identify and take appropriate actions and practice intervention skills. (Activities 4.6 *I Can Help By:*, 4.7 *I Will Do Something*, 4.8 *What Should I Say?* & 4.9 *Just Ask*.)
   - Provide help with assertiveness skills. (Activities 6.2 *Being Assertive Helps* & 6.3 *The "I Messages" Have It*.)
   - Make sure students know how and when to report bullying to the staff. (Unit One – *Reporting Bullying Behavior*.)
   - Instruct students in ways to deal with their feelings of helplessness and guilt when they witness bullying. (Activities 4.10 *Defeat Evil*, 4.11 *How Would You Feel?*, 4.12 *We Have Rights and Responsibilities*, 6.6 *Changing Self-Defeating Behaviors*, 6.7 *Sticks and Stones*, 6.8 *My Feelings Are Important* & 6.9 *It's Not Fair*.)
   - Encourage students to develop their own character through helping someone else. (Unit One – *Friendship Teams* & *Opportunities for Community Service*)

4. Include conflict resolution and mediation training in the curriculum for students. (Activities 4.14 *We Have Different Ideas*, 4.15 *Conflicts Have Two Sides* & 4.16 *Mediation Works*)

5. Create an appreciation for diversity among students. (Unit One – *Promote Equity and Respect, Mix It Up At Lunch*, Activities 4.17 *Strength From Diversity* & Unit Six – *Instruction on Disabilities*.)

6. Teach students to value non-violence and peace. (Activities 4.18 *The Nobel Peace Prize* & 4.19 *Violence in Your Life*)

LET'S DISCUSS BULLYING
Activity 4.1

Purpose
To gain information from students on their feelings concerning bullying.
To help students develop a concern for both the bully and the victim.

Materials
Chalk board, chart or overhead.

Procedure
Introduce the topic of bullying by reviewing what you have (or the school has) done so far on the topic. Tell the students that this is going to be an open discussion of bullying to help you (and/or the school) understand how students feel about bullying and assess what their needs are. Try to present a neutral opinion-gathering attitude while trying to elicit positive and constructive suggestions from the students. Encourage students to share their feelings openly and remind them that you want to hear from everyone. Encourage the students to be respectful of everyone's opinions. You will want to write each of the questions on the board or overhead, under each question record student responses. Discuss the following questions.

- What allows bullying to occur?
- What types of things do bullies do at our school?
- How does it make you feel when you see someone being bullied?
- How do you think bullying makes the victim feel?
- How does bullying make the bully feel?

Follow-up
Ask the Students:
- Can bullying be stopped?
- Is it fair for the bully to make everyone feel bad?
- What else could bullies do to make themselves feel powerful other than bullying?
- How do you feel about bullying?

BULLYING IS ABOUT POWER
Activity 4.2

Purpose
To help students understand a bully's use of power.

Materials
Chalk board, chart or overhead

Procedure
Make this statement to your students: "Bullying is always inflicted by a more powerful person against a less powerful one." Ask the students if they agree or disagree with this statement. Explain that bullies need to feel powerful and that controlling other people's behavior or emotions makes them feel powerful. Bullies always look for someone they believe is weaker than they are.

Ask the students: In what ways can a person be more powerful than another? Begin to list the suggestions on the board (overhead). Your list should include the following ways a person can be more powerful:

> Physically (you can be bigger or stronger);
> Socially (you can be more popular);
> Aesthetically (you can be more physically attractive);
> Economically (you can have more money/better car/clothes/stuff/etc.);
> Academically (you can be smarter or more successful);
> Age (if all else fails, pick on someone younger).

Discuss with the students how each of these types of power can be used to bully.

Follow-up
Ask the students:
- Can people have power in these areas and not abuse it?
- Can people of equal power tease each other on occasion and it is not bullying? (Example – Can two football players punch each other in the arm and it not be bullying?)
- What makes abuse of power so wrong?
- Can you think of examples in history where people abused power?
- How can people feel more powerful without resorting to bullying?

WRITE ABOUT BULLYING
Activity 4.3

Purpose
To gain anecdotal information about bullying from students.
To allow students an outlet to express their feelings and attitudes.

Materials
Paper and pencil/pen

Procedure
Ask the students to write an essay about a bullying incident that occurred between students at their school. Stress that this can be something that happened to them or something they witnessed. The essays should NOT include the names of the people involved in the bullying incidents. You may want to provide a name bank for students to use. Identify names that are not common at your school.

This can be part of an English lesson or an extra credit assignment. If this lesson is being used as a class assignment, make the following decisions concerning the essay and inform the students prior to their beginning the assignment.

- Does the student have to include their name on the essay or is it optional?
- Will the assignment be graded and if so, what will be the criteria for grading?
- Does the student have the right to request that their essay not be read as part of the follow-up discussion and how should they indicate that they do not want it read aloud?

Give students time to write their essays during class or make it a homework assignment.

Follow-up
Because this could be an overnight or long assignment the follow-up should probably be saved for another day. Collect the essays and select those that will lead to good discussion. You will probably want to select essays that represent examples of different types of bullying and describe different situations. Follow the procedure on Activity 4. 4 *Read About Bullying*.

READ ABOUT BULLYING
Activity 4.4

Purpose
To facilitate discussion of bullying.
To encourage students to develop an understanding of the problem of bullying at their school.

Materials
Selected essays from Activity 4.3

Procedure
Select essays from Activity 4.3 that you feel are appropriate for classroom discussion. Choose essays that represent different styles of bullying (threats, embarrassment, isolation, etc.) and bullying in different settings. Avoid essays where the bully and/or victim could be easily identified.

Large group – Before class, ask the student who wrote the essay if he/she wants to read the essay to the class or will allow you or another student to read it instead. Use the follow-up questions. Discuss as many essays as possible.

Small group – Divide the class into small groups of four or five. Make sure the groups are randomly selected. Give each group a different essay to read and review using the follow-up questions. Allow the groups time for their review. Bring the class back together and have each group report on its essay.

Follow-up
Ask the students:
- Who is the bully; what does he/she do? Who is the victim; what does he/she do? Who are the bystanders; how do they respond?
- What type of bullying is taking place?
- What is the bully's goal?
- What could the bully do differently to reach his/her goal?
- What could the victim have done that would have been more effective?
- What could the bystanders have done to defuse the situation and/or support the victim?

SHOULD I HELP?
Activity 4.5

Purpose
To help students determine whether they should intervene in a bullying situation.

Materials
Student Handout – **Should I Help?**

Procedure
Tell the students that intervening in a bullying situation can be very difficult and even dangerous. Students will never be expected to intervene when the intervention would put them at physical risk. It is also important to intervene in a way that will help and not make the situation worse. We are going to review a process you can use to help make the decision of whether to ignore the situation, intervene or go get help.

Give students the **Should I Help?** handout and discuss the steps in the process with them. Use the following questions that are related to the items on the student handout.

1. **Is the person being physically and/or emotionally injured ?**
   - How can you tell if someone is being injured?
   - How important is an imbalance of power in determining if someone is being injured?
   - How would you feel if you were in that person's position?

2. **Do you understand the situation and what is going on?**
   - Was there any provocation or previous teasing by either student?
   - Do you know anything about the personality of either of the participants?
   - Are these people friends just having a disagreement or is there a chronic problem between them?
   - Is one of the participants trying to get the other one in trouble?

3. **Will I be safe if I intervene?**
   - Has there been any physical contact in the interaction?
   - Is there a weapon or anything that could be used as a weapon available to either participant?
   - Are either of the participants making physical threats or gestures?
   - How could you create a diversion to distract people from a possibly violent confrontation?

4. **Do I have the skills to help?**
   - Can I speak up and tell the bully to stop?
   - Can I encourage the victim to leave and ignore the bully?
   - Should I create a disturbance to direct attention away from the situation?

5. **Will my intervention make things better?**
   - How could your intervention potentially make things worse?
   - Could you possibly get in trouble if your intervention was not appropriate and made the situation worse?

Follow-up
Ask the students:
- How can you use these steps to help you make a good decision concerning intervening in a bullying situation?
- Are there other things you would personally consider before intervening in a bullying situation?
- Who are some of the adults you could go to for help?

Should I Help?

When you are faced with a situation where you think bullying may be taking place, ask yourself the following questions before you intervene. If the answer to the question is no, follow the suggestions. If the answer to all of the questions is yes, then you should intervene.

1. Is the person being injured physically and/or emotionally?

No – Ignore

Yes – Go to the next question.

2. Do you fully understand the situation and what is going on?

No – Get an adult to help.

Yes – Go to the next question.

3. Will I be safe if I intervene?

No – Get an adult to help or create a diversion.

Yes – Go to the next question.

4. Do I have the skills to help?

No – Get an adult to help.

Yes – Go to the next question.

5. Will my intervention make things better?

No – Get an adult to help.

Yes – Intervene.

I CAN HELP BY:
Activity 4.6

Purpose
To help students identify intervention strategies.

Materials
Student handout – *I Can Help By:*
This handout will also be used for Activity 4.7

Procedure
Tell the students that there are many different appropriate responses when they see someone being bullied. Remind the students that no one expects or wants them to put themselves in a situation where they may be physically hurt, but that everyone is still expected to respond appropriately.

Give the students the *I Can Help By:* handout. Go over the handout with the students discussing how and when each intervention might be used.

- **Not spreading rumors.** When students refuse to participate in rumors, the rumors will stop. Discuss electronic bullying in relation to rumors (*School Strategies – Evaluate the Problem of Bullying*).
  How do rumors fuel bullying?
  How can you respond when a rumor is passed to you?

- **Refusing to join in when someone is being bullied.** Bullies depend on support from bystanders to maintain their power. If bullies do not get any support from bystanders, their power is greatly limited.
  Ask the students:
  How do bystanders often enable the bully to have power?
  What ways can you demonstrate your lack of support for the bully?

- **Getting a staff member to assist during a bullying situation.** Alert the closest staff member to what is going on and enable them to intervene and stop the incident.
  Ask the students:
  What are some situations where you should immediately alert an adult?
  How do students protect a bully through silence?

- **Reporting the bullying to an adult.** Make a report to an adult even if the bullying situation has ended. Ask the students:
  Why would you report the incident if the bullying situation has ended?
  Who are some of the adults you could inform about the bullying?

- **Creating a distraction to draw attention away from the bullying.** Bullies like to be the center of attention. When you draw attention away, the bullying may stop.
  Ask the students:
  What are some things you could do or say to distract the bully?
  (Drop your books; announce that a teacher is coming; ignore what is happening and ask the bully or victim a question; remind them that class is about to start; etc.)

I CAN HELP BY:

Activity 4.6 <small>(continued)</small>

- **Being kind to the victim of bullying.** Victims of bullying often feel rejected and lonely. Acts of kindness from other students can be healing for emotional wounds caused by bullying.
  > Ask the students:
  > What are some ways you can be kind to a student who has been bullied?

- **Speaking up when I see someone being bullied.** Students can directly intervene and stop the bullying. But remind them, never bully the bully. Ask the students:
  > What can you do to intervene when you see bullying?
  > How can you get the bully to stop without making threats?

Follow-up

Ask the students:

- Which of these strategies would be the most difficult? The easiest?
- What keeps most students from intervening when they witness bullying?
- If all students made a commitment to use the strategies we have discussed today, what difference would it make at our school?

I CAN HELP BY:

1. **Not spreading rumors.**

2. **Refusing to join in when someone is being bullied.**

3. **Getting a staff member to assist during a bullying situation.**

4. **Reporting the bullying to an adult.**

5. **Creating a distraction to draw attention away from the bullying.**

6. **Being kind to the victim of bullying.**

7. **Speaking up when I see someone being bullied.**

I WILL DO SOMETHING
Activity 4.7

Purpose
To help students identify appropriate intervention strategies.

Materials
Student handout – *I Can Help By:* 4.6
Scenarios for Activity 4.7

Procedure
Tell the students that it is important to know when to use an intervention strategy. Give each of them a copy of the student handout *I Can Help By:* or provide the information on an overhead.

Divide the class into groups of five or six members each. Give each group one or more of the scenarios for this activity. Select scenarios that are appropriate for your students. Explain to the students that they are to identify all the strategies from the *I Can Help By:* handout and which ones that they might use for their scenario. Each group will be asked to role-play (all) the interventions they selected for the class. Remind the students that different people might respond differently and that is okay.

Allow the groups time to select their interventions and prepare their role-plays.

Follow-up
Ask the students:
* How do you think other students would react to you if you intervened in some of the ways we have discussed today?
* What makes students do nothing about bullying?
* Where is most of this pressure coming from?
* What is the hardest part about intervening when someone is being bullied?

SCENARIOS FOR ACTIVITY 4.7

- John is teasing Perry about his recent hair cut.

- Tyler intentionally trips Adam in the hall, calls him clumsy and laughs.

- Amber doesn't want to be friends with Jane and asks everyone else to ignore her too.

- For several days you have observed Sam taking Matt's pencil during math class. He does it again today.

- LaShanda is teasing Erin because she often wears the same pair of jeans. Other people are looking, and Erin is obviously embarrassed.

- Tyron has heard that some of the boys are going to beat him up during P.E. He showed you the knife he brought to school for protection.

- Teresa tells you about a web site that lists all the boys that Sarah has "been with." She encourages you to visit the site.

- Michael accidentally bumps into Hunter in the hallway. Hunter gets angry and starts making threatening comments and actions toward Michael.

- Julie is eating lunch in the cafeteria when Lisa tells her she needs to move to another table because Lisa and her friends always sit at that table.

- You notice that Ben has bruises on his arm. When you ask him what happened, he reluctantly tells you that Justin punches him in the arm every day when they are going into science class.

- Linda gives you a note that says that Katie is fat, stupid and ugly, and no one is going to sit with her. She wants you to sign the note to show your agreement. There are already several signatures on the note.

- Caleb is often teased by classmates because he has difficulty reading and has poor grades. He leaves a note in your locker telling you he just can't take it any more and he thanks you for always being nice to him.

WHAT SHOULD I SAY?

Activity 4.8

Purpose
To help students make good decisions when intervening in bullying situations.

Materials
Student handout – *What Should I Say?*

Procedure
Tell the students that when you witness bullying, there are numerous responses each of us can have. While it is always wrong to encourage bullies and give them support by joining in with their bullying, there are many options you can choose that will let the bully know you do not like his/her behavior.

Give students the **What Should I Say?** handout and explain the directions. Remind the students that the response they choose should be respectful and non-violent. Allow students to choose their responses.

After students have independently completed the handout, lead a discussion of their responses. Ask, "Who chose the first response?" Have students share why they chose that particular response. Continue to ask students who chose the 2nd, then 3rd responses and discuss why they preferred that response. There is one "wrong" response in each group of responses. Discuss why that response would be inappropriate.

Follow-up
Ask the students:
- What made some responses seem more comfortable to you than others?
- What makes it hard to directly confront bullies about their behavior?
- What makes some of the responses inappropriate?

WHAT SHOULD I SAY?

Review each of the following situations. Put an X by the response you would feel the most comfortable using.

1. You are eating lunch in the cafeteria with several friends when Joshua walks by and grabs french fries from Joe's tray. Joe doesn't say anything but looks hurt and upset. Joshua just laughs and grabs more french fries. You could say:
   - ❑ "Joshua, if you don't stop, I'm going to punch you out!"
   - ❑ "Joshua, that's not funny. You need to leave Joe alone."
   - ❑ "We know you are hungry Joshua, but leave Joe's lunch alone."

2. You are talking with friends when Kim, a new student from another country, joins your group. Ann says, "This is a private conversation. No foreigners allowed." You could say:
   - ❑ "Ann, that's not the way we all feel. Kim, you are welcome to stay."
   - ❑ "Ann, who put you in charge of our group?"
   - ❑ "Kim, I was going to get some water; why don't you come with me."

3. You are in the hall between classes when Ray accidentally bumps into Bill causing Bill to drop his books. Bill starts screaming at Ray and demands Ray pick up his books. Ray refuses. You could say:
   - ❑ "Come on Bill calm down; it was just an accident."
   - ❑ "Are you going to let him get away with that Bill?"
   - ❑ "It's no big deal Bill; I'll help you pick up the books."

4. Karen tells you that she heard Wendy had head lice and that is why she has been out of school. Karen reports that none of the girls are going to let her sit with them at lunch. You could say:
   - ❑ "Karen, that's just a rumor, and you shouldn't be spreading rumors."
   - ❑ "Wendy is my friend, and if you do that, I will tell everyone that you have herpes."
   - ❑ "Karen, that is mean. I don't care what the rest of you do, but I am going to sit with Wendy at lunch."

5. The class is working on group projects. In your group, Luke keeps daring Juan to glue the teacher's book to her desk. Juan has ADHD and is getting wound up. You could say:
   - ❑ "Luke, knock it off. We've got to get this project finished."
   - ❑ "Juan, don't listen to him; he just wants to get you into trouble."
   - ❑ "Do it, Juan. That would be so funny."

6. Jane always wears the latest and most expensive fashions. In the dressing room before P.E., she starts teasing Linda who is obviously wearing inexpensive tennis shoes. You could say:
   - ❑ "Linda, just ignore her. Let's go on to P.E."
   - ❑ "Jane, you are being rude. Just leave Linda alone."
   - ❑ "Jane, you are so stuck up. Go look at your reflection in the mirror and leave Linda alone."

JUST ASK
Activity 4.9

Purpose
To teach students to be assertive when they witness bullying.

Materials
Student Handout – *Just Ask*

Procedure
Tell the students that one strategy to use with bullies is to just ask them to stop the behavior. If a bully realizes that their behavior is not being supported by the other students, they are less likely to continue the behavior. Remind the students that it is NEVER acceptable to bully the bully. Even if the bully stops their behavior because of threats, the disrespect continues. Student's witnessing bulling need to ask the bully to stop his/her behavior in a firm, calm voice.

Give each student a copy of the student handout. Ask them to read each scenario and write a response. After the students have completed their responses, divide the class in groups of 6 to 8 students. In these groups each person is to share his/her responses with the group and the group will choose the best response to share with the class. Encourage the groups to have as many good responses as they can to share.

When the groups have selected their best response, bring the class back together and have the groups share these responses with the entire class. Select one group to share a response to the first situation. Ask the other groups if they have any different responses. Select another group to share a response to the second situation and continue until you have discussed all the scenarios.

Follow-up
Ask the students:
* Have you ever witnessed a situation similar to these and not spoken up?
  What makes you not say anything?
* What is the hardest part about speaking up when you see someone being bullied?
* Do you think other students would support you if you intervened to stop bullying?

JUST ASK

Read each of these scenarios. Think of a way to respond to the bully. Make sure your responses are respectful. Write your response in the space provided.

Kevin is eating his lunch in the cafeteria. Tyron opens a pack of ketchup and deliberately squirts it on Kevin. Kevin looks embarrassed and hurt. He doesn't say anything to Tyron. Tyron starts laughing. **You could say...**

_____

_____

_____

You are sitting at the lunch table with Wanda and some other friends. Wanda tells everyone at the table, "When Sandy comes to the table today, lets tell her she can't sit with us." **You could say...**

_____

_____

_____

Juanita is a new student at your school. When she tries to join your group to work on a project, Tom says "We don't need you in our group, find another group." **You could say...**

_____

_____

_____

Jim has never been good in sports. He made several mistakes during the ball game during P.E. On the way back to class Adam walks behind him saying unkind things about his lack of skill. Jim just keeps walking and tries to ignore Adam, but Adam is getting louder. **You could say...**

_____

_____

_____

DEFEAT EVIL
Activity 4.10

Purpose
To encourage students take action when they see bullying.

Materials
Overhead or poster with Burke's quote.

Procedure
Present this Edmond Burke quote to the class by writing it on the board or presenting it on an overhead.

The only thing necessary for the triumph of evil is for good people to do nothing.

— Edmond Burke

Lead a class discussion with reference to the quote asking questions such as:

What do you think this quote means?
- Do you agree with the quote? Why or why not?
- Can you think of situations from the past that might relate to this quote?
- Can you think of situations today that might relate to this quote?
- How does this quote relate to the subject of bullying?

Divide the class into groups of three to five. Instruct each group to write a poem or short story with the title "I Will Do Something." Instruct the students to remember the discussion of the quote. The group's story or poem should include references telling how actions can impact bullying in school. Tell the groups to plan how they will present their poem or story to the class.

Inform the groups of how much time they have to complete their assignment. Allow time for each group to present their product to the class. You may want to post some of the poems or stories around the room.

Follow-up
Ask the students:
- Is bullying evil? Why or why not?
- Can staff members stop bullying in our school?
- What will it take for bullying to be truly stopped in our school?

HOW WOULD YOU FEEL?
Activity 4.11

Purpose
To foster empathy for others.
To help students identify feelings.

Materials
Student handout – *How Would You Feel?*

Procedure
Children are born with a tendency toward showing empathy to others. For this tendency to grow, it must be nurtured and encouraged. Tell the students that while all of us are different in many ways we all have the same feelings and need to be accepted. In order for us to work together it is important to be able to think about how other people feel and how our actions affect others.

Give each student the handout, *How Would You Feel?* Instruct the students to write how they would feel if they were in this situation, by the statements. You can identify more than one feeling word. Have the students complete the handout.

Bring the class back together. Read each statement and have students share their responses. Discuss student responses and identify as many feelings as you can. After you have identified how a person would feel, ask "If that is the way you feel, how would you act?" Continue to review all the items on the handout in the identifying actions related to feelings.

Follow-up
Ask the students:
* Does everyone always have the same feelings in the same situation?
* What are other factors that affect our feelings?
* How do feelings affect our behaviors?
* Did your feelings about some statements change when the next statement informed you that you were being teased about a quality?
* Can teasing turn a neutral or even positive quality into a negative experience?

HOW WOULD YOU FEEL?

We are different in many ways and we all have different feelings. Beside each of these situations, describe how you would feel if you were in that situation.

1. You are new at school. _____

    _____

2. You are the tallest student in the class. _____

    _____

3. People tease you about being tall. _____

    _____

4. You are the last picked for a sports team. _____

    _____

5. You are not a good reader. _____

    _____

6. People tease you when you read aloud. _____

    _____

7. You wear glasses. _____

    _____

8. Someone picks on you for wearing glasses. _____

    _____

9. You never have anyone to sit with at lunch. _____

    _____

10. People make fun of your clothes. _____

    _____

WE HAVE RIGHTS AND RESPONSIBILITIES
Activity 4.12

Purpose
To help students identify their rights.
To help students identify their responsibilities to others.

Materials
Chalk board, chart or overhead

Procedure
Rights and responsibilities are the hallmark of our democratic society. Students need to recognize early the relationship between the two. Tell the students that as American citizens we have rights. These rights are stated in the "Bill of Rights" which is the first 10 amendments to the Constitution. As students we also have rights and today we are going to create our own "Bill of Rights."

Ask the students "What are our basic rights in this classroom (school)?" As students offer suggestions begin writing them on the board or chart. If students make suggestions that are inappropriate (sit where ever you want), discuss the problem with them and have the class make the decision to eliminate them. You may want to try to have 10 items on your list but that is not required. Your list should include items such as:

- Right to learn
- Right to be different
- Right to be left alone
- Right to be included
- Right to be treated with respect

After you have an agreement on what should be included on the "Bill of Rights." Tell the students that all rights come with responsibilities. Ask the students "If these are the rights of everyone in this room (school), what are our responsibilities to each other?" Begin making a list of responsibilities that students need to assume so everyone will be able to enjoy their rights. The responsibilities will identify specific behaviors students will need to follow for the rights to be manifested. Examples of what your list should include:

- Responsibility to do your assignments
- Responsibility to not disturb the learning of others
- Responsibility to respect differences
- Responsibility to treat others with respect

Make posters stating the rights and responsibilities of students to display in the classroom.

Follow-up
Ask the students:
- What makes it important for us to have a "Bill of Rights" for students?
- What should we do if someone is violating our rights?
- How are our rights and responsibilities related to each other?
- If everyone acted responsibly, would everyone be able to enjoy their rights?

LET'S BE FRIENDS
Activity 4.13

Purpose
To have students identify what makes a good friend.
To have students identify behaviors that hurt friendships.
To help students realize that bullying can hurt a friendship.

Materials
Chalk board, chart or overhead

Procedure
Explain to the class that everyone needs friends and all of us can benefit from learning and practicing friendship skills. Tell the students that today we are going to look at what makes someone a good friend. Ask the students to think about their friends and name some of the qualities they like most about them. Write the heading "Friendship Do's" on the board and list the students' ideas in a column. If students make suggestions like "give you money" or "loan you things", discuss how at times loaning things can cause a friendship to break up (things get lost or damaged).

Next tell the students that we need to look at behaviors that can hurt a friendship or keep you from making friends. Write "Friendship Don'ts" on the board and encourage students to give examples of behaviors that keep you from making friends. Write this list parallel to the friendship list.

Follow-up
Ask the students:
* What are some of the suggestions on the friendship list that are easy to do?
* What are some of the suggestions that are hard? What makes them hard?
* Can you practice being a good friend? How?
* How could our classroom be different if we all practiced the "Friendship Do" skills?
* How can we let people know when they are not being a good friend without being mean to them?
* Can bullying ruin a friendship? How?
* Have everyone pick one "Friendship Do's" that they will especially work on this week.

WE HAVE DIFFERENT IDEAS
Activity 4.14

Purpose
To demonstrate that we all have different ideas.
To help students realize that conflict is normal and inevitable.

Materials
None

Procedure
Explain to the class that conflict between people is normal and inevitable. Conflicts arise because we all have different ideas, values and perceptions about the way things should be. Not all conflicts are harmful or bad. A conflict is destructive if it hurts relationships or creates bad feelings. Some conflicts help us learn about each other and can help us change for the better. When we listen to the ideas of others, we become more open-minded and tolerant.

Designate each corner of the room as a one of these choices: strongly agree, agree, disagree and strongly disagree. Tell the class, I am going to read a statement you are to move to the corner that best expresses your opinion about the statement.

Read each statement and allow students time to move. After everyone has moved into position, ask for a volunteer(s) from each corner to share their reasons for selecting a particular stand. Inform the students after they have listened to other student's choices, that they can change corners if they wish.

Use these statements or make similar statement that may be more age appropriate.

- It is better to work at a job that pays a lot of money even if you don't enjoy the job.
- Everyone should go to college; technical schools are just for losers.
- You should be able to date anyone you like, even if your parents tell you "no."
- The military is a great way to get training after high school.

Follow-up
Ask the Students:
- Were you influenced by the choices others in the class made?
- Did you feel a need to make everyone agree with you on an issue? Why or why not?
- Were you swayed by the opinions of others in the group and change your opinion on an issue?
- Is it good to have different opinions on issues? Why?
- What would happen if we all had the same opinion about these issues?

CONFLICTS HAVE TWO SIDES
Activity 4.15

Purpose
To practice analyzing conflicts to determine both sides of the issue.
To practice finding solutions to conflicts that can be agreeable to both sides.

Materials
Student handout – **Conflicts Have Two Sides**

Procedure
Explain to the class that some conflicts cause people to say angry words, insults and even resort to physical violence. When people have strong feelings, feelings can block their ability to search for a reasonable and logical solution. Resolving a conflict is helped when each person can acknowledge the strong feelings they have and recognize the feelings of the other(s) involved.

Divide the class into random groups with 4 or 5 members. Give each group a copy of the **Conflicts Have Two Sides** handout. Instruct each group to identify the opposing positions and come up with suggestions of possible solutions that could be agreeable to both.

Bring the class together and allow each group to share their solutions to the conflict.

Follow-up
Ask the students:
* Is it more or less difficult to see both sides of a conflict when you are not involved? Why?
* How did each person's feelings affect their responses?
* Does identifying feelings make conflicts easier to resolve? Why?
* How can having a third person, who is not involved in the conflict, help to settle the conflict?

CONFLICTS HAVE TWO SIDES

Robin and Jean have been best friends for three years. They spend a lot of time together but they don't share all the same interests. Robin is really into sports and likes to go to all the football games. Jean doesn't care for football and often gets upset with Robin when she goes to games with her other friends. Jean has been waiting for months for a certain movie to come to the local theater. She wants to go see the movie on opening day. When she reminds Robin of the date of the movie, Robin tells her she is going to the football game that night and can't go with her. Jean gets furious and tells Robin that a real friend would know how important this movie was and would skip the game this one time. Robin points out that this is the last game of the year and Jean shouldn't expect her to miss it. Jean calls Robin selfish and storms away.

Robin's position: _____

_____

Robin's feelings: _____

_____

_____

Jean's position: _____

_____

Jean's feelings: _____

_____

_____

Possible solutions: _____

_____

_____

_____

MEDIATION WORKS
Activity 4.16

Purpose
To teach the mediation process.
To practice mediation.

Materials
Resolution Rules
Mediator Instructions
Mediation Role-plays
Mediation Report Form

Procedure
Tell the students that mediation can be a simple, fair way to resolve a conflict. A mediator is a third person who is trained to lead the mediation sessions and not take sides. The mediator is to help both sides listen to each other and reach an agreement. If your school has or plans to start a peer mediation program, you can explain how your students can seek mediation or apply to be trained as a mediator. If the counselor or other school personnel are identified as mediators, inform the students how to ask for help. For more information on Peer Mediation you can contact the National Peer Helpers Association (NPHA).

Display the **Resolution Rules** and review them with the students. Tell the students that we can all learn about conflict resolution by going through the mediation process. Divide the students into groups of 3 or 4 members. Two students will role-play the students having the conflict and the other student(s) will serve as the mediator. Give each group a copy of the **Resolution Rules**. Give a role-play situation to two students in each group and the **Mediator Instructions** and **Report Form** to the other student. If there is a fourth person in the group, ask them to observe the mediation and provide feedback to the other group members. Allow everyone time to review their roles. As time allows, rotate the roles and continue the activity with different scenarios until everyone has had an opportunity to be the mediator.

Follow-up
Ask the students:
- Why are the Resolution Rules important?
- Was it harder to role-play the conflict or be the mediator?
- Was it difficult to summarize what the other person said? Why do you think it was hard?
- Why is it difficult to settle a conflict in front of others?
- How can we use what we have learned about mediation to settle any conflict?

RESOLUTION RULES

1. Identify the problem.

2. Focus on the problem.

3. Listen without interrupting.

4. Accept responsibility for your actions.

5. Be respectful.

6. Solve the problem.

7. Make the solution work.

Mediators Instructions

As the mediator your role is to maintain order and assist the communication between the students with the conflict. You are not to take sides. Follow these steps and complete the **Mediation Report Form.**

- Introduce yourself and tell the students you are here to assist them with resolving their conflict. Ask the students the following questions and get their verbal agreement to each question before moving on.

  Do you want to solve your conflict?
  Are you willing to listen without interrupting?
  Do you promise to tell the truth?
  Will you be respectful to everyone?

- If students agree to these conditions begin completing the report form with names, type of conflict (check as many as are applicable) and place of conflict.

- Without letting anyone see, write a number between one and ten on the back of the report form. Allow each person to guess a number. After they have guessed, show them the number and inform them that the person closest to the number will go first (student "A").

- Explain to the students that they will each tell their side of the story using a specific format. You will give them the start of three sentences and they will complete them. Tell the students that after each person tells his/her side, the other person will be asked to summarize what has been said so he/she will need to pay attention. Review the sentences with the students then begin by saying **"I feel…"** and have student "A" complete the sentence. Continue with **"when you…"** and go on to **"and I want you to…"**

  I feel…
  When you…
  And I want you to …

- Now turn to the student "B" and ask him/her to summarize with the prompt **"You said…"** After he/she has finished his/her summary turn to "A" and ask, **"Is that what you said?"** If "A" is not satisfied with the summary, continue getting clarification until student "A" is satisfied. If the answer is yes continue and allow student "B" to answer the three questions and student "A" will summarize.

- As the mediator, summarize the main components of the conflict as you have heard it. If both students agree with your summary, write it on the report form.

- Now ask both students to think of possible solutions to the conflict. Ask **"How can this conflict be solved?"** You may want to write the suggestions on the back of the report form (this will give you a record of all the suggestions if you need to review them later.) Encourage both students to make suggestions. It is important that both people agree to do something. You may need to remind them of the rules they agreed to at the beginning of the mediation. Good solutions identify observable behaviors.

- When there is an agreement, complete the agreement part of the report form and have both students sign the form. Tell the students that their signature indicates their willingness to carry out the agreement. Make copies of the agreement. Give a copy to each student and keep one yourself.

- Ask the students if they can think of anything they can do differently in the future to prevent another conflict. Encourage both students to answer.

- Indicate whether the conflict was resolved and sign your name on the report form.

- Thank the students for participating in mediation. Encourage them to tell their friends the conflict has been resolved and to not do anything to create a new problem.

MEDIATION ROLE-PLAYS

Situation One

As people were coming into class, Dana left her bookbag on Jean's desk while she was turning in an assignment. Jean came to her desk and found someone else's bookbag there and picked it up to put it on the floor. Dana turned to see Jean about to drop the bag on the floor and rushed to her grabbing it from her hand. In the process of grabbing it from Jean's hand, the strap broke and all the books, papers, etc. spilled on the floor. Dana screams, "Look what you've done! You better pick everything up and I'm going to make you pay for the bag!" Jean screams back, "You're the one who broke the strap when you grabbed it! You shouldn't have left it on my desk. I'm not picking up anything!"

Situation Two

Maria and Joe are eating lunch in the cafeteria with several classmates. Joe was talking and laughing while he explained how he caught a fly ball at the game yesterday. As he was demonstrating his skill with the ball, his hand hit Maria's lunch tray, knocking it to the floor. Maria screams "You are so clumsy, look what you have done!" Joe, not wanting to be embarrassed, replies "Don't get in my way. Who asked you to come to this table anyway?" Maria announced "You are going to clean this up and buy me another lunch!" Joe replied "You're not telling me what to do."

Situation Three

Billy is in line to get lunch when he sees his friend come into the lunchroom. His friend had borrowed his math book, so Billy left his place in line to get the book and put it with his things at the lunch table. When Billy comes back to his former place in the line Tony won't allow him to get back in line. Tony said "Hey jerk, no butting in line!" Billy not feeling like he needed to explain said "I was here before you were." Tony, getting louder, said "Well you're not getting in front of me!" Billy feeling threatened retorted "What are you going to do about it?" Both students were getting angry and loud.

Situation Four

Lakisha and Samantha are friends. Lakisha tells Samantha that she likes Travis. That evening, Lakisha e-mails the news to Sam, who is one of Travis' friends. Sam forwards the e-mail to everyone on his e-mail list. The next day almost everyone in the class was teasing Lakisha about her feelings for Travis. Lakisha is furious and screams "Samantha you are a real blabber mouth. I'll never trust you again!" Lakisha tries to justify her behavior by saying "I told Sam it was a secret. How could I know he would send an e-mail to everyone?"

MEDIATION REPORT FORM

Date _____

Students Involved in the Conflict:

Name _____ Grade ___ Age___ ❑ Male ❑ Female

Name _____ Grade ___ Age___ ❑ Male ❑ Female

Others _____

Type of Conflict:

❑ Teasing   ❑ Friendship   ❑ Property   ❑ Fighting

❑ Name-calling   ❑ Rumors   ❑ Threats

Other _____

Place of Conflict:

❑ Classroom   ❑ P.E.   ❑ Internet/electronic

❑ Restroom   ❑ Cafeteria   ❑ Other _____

❑ Hall/lockers   ❑ Campus

Describe the Conflict:

_____

_____

_____

_____

Agreements:

_____ Agrees to and _____ Agrees to

_____.

Signature _____

Signature _____

Conflict Resolved? _____   Mediator _____

142

STRENGTH FROM DIVERSITY
Activity 4.17

Purpose
To help all students evaluate their personal feelings about diversity.
To improve contact and understanding among students of different groups.

Materials
Student handout – *The Content of My Character*
Overhead or poster with Dr. Kings quote.

Procedure
Have students complete the handout – *The Content of My Character* without discussion or comment. Instruct the students to answer, based on their first reaction. Assure the students that they will **not** have to share the content of their survey with others. When students have completed the survey, ask them to hold them for later discussion.

Present the following excerpt from Dr. Martin Luther King Jr. famous *I Have a Dream Speech* delivered at the Lincoln memorial, Washington, D.C., August 28, 1963. You could use an overhead or make a poster that could be displayed in the classroom.

"I have a dream that my four children will one day live in a nation where they will not be judged by the color of their skin, but the content of their character."

Tell the students that Dr. King had a dream and a vision for America. In 1963 there was injustice, racism and oppression in our country and in our schools. Ask the students:
- How have things changed in schools, transportation and employment since Dr. King made his speech?
- Do injustice, racism and oppression still exist in America? In our school? Give examples.

Have the students review their answers to the handout they completed at the beginning of the lesson. Inform the students that "No" answers represent a tendency toward prejudice and exclusion. Ask the students:
- After discussing Dr. Kings comments, are you satisfied with the results of your survey?
- What have you learned about yourself?
- What can you do to change the situation?

Follow-up
Challenge your students to choose one of the statements from the handout that they would like to change. Dare them to have the courage to make a conscious effort to take steps to change their behavior and act with more character.

You may want to follow-up this activity with one of the activities from Unit Two which are designed to help students get to know each other (Activities 2.1 and 2.5). While these activities are designed to help students get better acquainted, you may want to deliberately use them with students of different racial and ethnic backgrounds.

THE CONTENT OF MY CHARACTER

Respond to each of the following questions by circling the response that you agree with.

1. I treat people of all racial, religious and ethnic groups with respect.

   Yes   **No**

2. I have friends of different racial, religious and ethnic backgrounds.

   Yes   **No**

3. I often eat lunch with people of different racial, religious and ethnic groups.

   Yes   **No**

4. I treat people as individuals rather than as members of specific groups.

   Yes   **No**

5. I do not judge people based on the way they look, how they dress or how they speak.

   Yes   **No**

6. I try to get to know the people who look, dress or speak differently from me.

   Yes   **No**

7. There are groups in our school that appear to get favorite treatment?

   Yes   **No**

8. There are groups in our school who are ignored and are considered outcast.

   Yes   **No**

9. There are groups in our school who I ignore and consider as outcast.

   Yes   **No**

THE NOBEL PEACE PRIZE
Activity 4.18

Purpose
To help students learn more about peacemakers.

Materials
Students will need access to resource materials.

Procedure
Explain to the students that the **Nobel Peace Prize** is awarded to the man or woman who has done the most to advance the idea of international peace, regardless of nationality. Alfred Bernhard Nobel was a Swedish chemist who invented dynamite. Within a few years, Nobel became one of the world's richest men. In later years, Nobel became distressed that his invention was used for war purposes and was responsible for the death of many people. His friend, Bertha Kinsky, who was very active in the Austrian Peace Society, urged him to use some of his money for peaceful purposes. Nobel liked the idea so much that he set up a fund, which makes it possible to give the Peace Prize every year to an outstanding individual who is working for peace.

You can have students complete this as a homework assignment. Provide resource information in your classroom or take your class to visit the library. Have students work in groups or individually to learn more about the men and women who have been awarded the **Nobel Peace Prize**. Student reports can be written or just given orally from notes.

Tell the students:
Select one of these men and women to research. You will report to the class on what you have found. You will need to report:

What year they received their award;
What country they represent;
What methods they used to accomplish their goals;
What were some of their accomplishments?

Select from this list of Nobel Peace Prize winners.

Jane Addams	Mairead Corrigan	Eisaku Saturday	Lech Walesa
Oscar Arias	Martin Luther King Jr.	Mother Teresa	Elie Wiesel
Ralph Bunche	Nelson Mandela	Le Duc Thos	Betty Williams
Jimmy Carter	Anwar Sadat	Desmond Tutu	

Follow-up
Have your students' present information they discovered concerning the Nobel Peace Prize winners.

VIOLENCE IN YOUR LIFE
Activity 4.19

Purpose
To help students become aware of the violence in their lives.

Materials
Paper and pencil
Parts of this activity may require students to visit stores, rent videos, or watch specific TV programs. Adapt the activity to the interest of your groups.

Procedure
Tell the students that there is research to show that TV programs, video games, toys, movies that glorify violence and war may cause students to become more aggressive and violent.

Present the following statistics to the students.
USA Today published a report in June or 1995 dealing with TV and violence.
* The average child watches up to 8,000 made-for-television murders and 100,000 acts of violence n television by the end of the 6th grade.

Ask the students:
* What impact do you think television violence has on you? America?
* Do you think you are exposed to an excessive amount of violence?

Ask the students to participate in some research of their own to evaluate their exposure to violence. Instruct the students to get out paper and a pencil.

Ask the students to:
* List three people they consider heroes;
* Name their three favorite video games;
* Identify their three favorite movies;
* Record their three favorite TV programs;
* List their three favorite toys.

After students have made their list, ask them to share their responses and come to an agreement on the most popular heroes, games, movies, toys and TV programs.

Have each student select at least one of the people, games, movies, toys or programs to research and report back to the class. Help students select a topic that they can easily research without renting the movie or watching a TV program their parents do not want them to watch.

If the student selected a **hero** to report on, have him research the person and report on things such as the hero's occupation, life style and positive and negative impact on youth. Has the hero had problems with the law? Does the hero give some of his/her time and money to positive causes etc.?

If the student is reporting on a **video game**, they will need to play the game and report on the amount of violence in the game. What is the goal of the game? How graphic is the violence?

If the student is reporting on a **TV show or movie**, she should watch the movie or program and report back to the class on the violence and aggression she observed. Is there use of profanity or aggressive language in the program or movie? Do the characters use nonviolent solutions etc.? You may also want to examine sexual content if you feel it is appropriate for your group.

If the student is reporting on a **toy**, they can bring the toy (if permitted) and explain what the main function of the toy is and why they enjoy the toy. What age group is the toy recommended for? Can the toy be used in violent or aggressive ways? If your students are older and you want to include toys in your research, have students go to a toy store and survey the toys being sold. Have them make a list of toys which are destructive/war-like and a list of toys which are challenging, creative, educational and nonviolent.

Follow-up
Have the students present their findings to the class.

Ask the students:
- In what areas that we examined did we find the most negative influences?
- In what areas that we examined did we find the most positive influences?
- What information presented was the most surprising to you?
- What are some other sources of violence that people are exposed to in our society?
- What are some ways that we can reduce our exposure to violence?

Unit Five
Learning a Better Way – Skills for Bullies

LEARNING A BETTER WAY: SKILLS FOR THE BULLY

**Treat a man as he is
and he will remain as he is.**

**Treat a man as he can
and should be
and he will become
as he can and should be.**

– Goethe (1749-1832), German Poet and Novelist

WHO ARE THESE BULLIES AND WHY DO THEY BULLY?

Bullies value power and the rewards achieved from being aggressive. When bullies control their victim's behavior and/or emotions, they feel they have power over the victim. Power can make the bullies feel better about themselves. A bully's positive self-image usually reflects a strong need for power and control. They feel that if they are bigger, louder, meaner, or angrier, people will do what they want. Bullies feel justified in hurting someone over and over again. They imagine power makes them stand out from the crowd and they often enjoy the attention their aggressive behavior brings. They often have positive, sometimes unrealistic, self images. They feel the need to dominate in situations by threats and intimidation rather than reasoning power. Using bullying to gain power is very destructive to everyone involved.

Bullies usually start out as smart as other students, but by the 6th grade they start to fall behind in school. Because of their aggressive behaviors, bullies have more suspensions and detentions. Students identified as bullies drop out of school in higher numbers. Since bullies are usually not model students, they do not experience positive relationships with their teachers. Teachers should work to establish a positive, friendly, and trusting relationship with the aggressive, disruptive students who may have had negative experiences with adults. It is easier for students to accept criticism and positive instruction if they feel the teacher cares about them. Teachers have a great opportunity to bring the bully into the mainstream of the school and help them gain power in positive ways.

While bullies are sometimes viewed positively by their peers, they are rarely capable of maintaining close friendships. It is more common for bullies to have a network of peers who encourage, admire, and model their bullying behavior. These relationships are often based on the idea that if they are friends with the bully, they won't be the victim of his bullying. Non-offending students must stop supporting students that employ bulling behaviors to gain popularity.

Leonard Eron, a psychology professor at the *University of Michigan*, has studied aggressive children for more than 30 years. He concludes: that while there is a genetic component to some aggressive behavior, bullying is largely a learned behavior. Bullying can be the results of viewing aggression on television and video games but it is more likely the results of having parents who are bullies themselves. Eron's research shows that children who bully often grow up to be adult bullies and often live very unhappy lives. He found that children who were aggressive at age 8 continued to be aggressive at age 19 and at age 30. Studies have found that children as young a 2 begin to pick up bullying habits. The longer a behavior continues, the harder it is to change. Early intervention is critical. Bullies can be taught non-violent behaviors at school even when aggression is modeled and reinforced at home.

Students identified as bullies are more likely to have troubled backgrounds. They are more likely to have family problems and a history of physical or emotional abuse. There is often a lack of parental warmth and involvement and inconsistent discipline at home. The *British Medical Journal* released the results of a 1999 study surveying 16,410 adolescents aged 14-16. The study revealed an increased incidence of depression and severe suicidal ideation among both those who were bullied and those who were bullies. While depression occurred equally among the bully and victims, suicidal ideation occurred most often among adolescents who were bullies. Bullying may actually be a cry for help.

BULLYING BOYS AND GIRLS

There are differences between boys and girls when it comes to bullying. A majority of bullying is perpetrated by males, whether against males or females. 10% of males are identified as bullies and about 4% of the female population according the *Center for Disease Control* statistics (2001). They also indicate that the fastest growing type of bullying is female to female. In 2003, the *National Institute of Child Health and Human Development* surveyed 15,686 students in grades six through ten. They reported that boys were more likely to be involved in bullying and violent behavior than were girls.

Both boys and girls bully, but their tactics are usually different. Boys are upfront and usually bully with physical aggression or threats. They seem to end their arguments in one way, fighting. Boys wage physical warfare where girls are more likely to use psychological attacks. Our culture has historically discouraged girls from using open conflict and they are forced into indirect and covert forms of aggression. Girls are sneaky and are more likely to use exclusion, rumors, name-calling and manipulation against their targets. Another distinct difference between the bullying of boys and girls, is that boys tend to bully acquaintances or strangers while girls often target friends. Just when you think a girl is your friend she attacks. Girls don't even have to use lies, they use information entrusted to them which can intensify the damage to their victims.

Male bullies often want to live out the tough guy image and feel it is proper. The *Josephson Institute of Ethics* conducted a study in 2001. They report that 43% of high school and 37% of middle school boys believe it is okay to hit or threaten a person who makes them angry. In the same study only 19% of the girls agreed that hitting was acceptable. Male bullies usually get their bullying traits from an older adult role model such as a father or brother. Bullying and its violence can carry over into all areas of their lives. In a Washington, D.C. study of juvenile violence, 82% of the most violent crimes were committed by males. Males were significantly more likely than females to bully their peers and twice as likely as females to engage in physical actions to bully others. Is it any wonder then, that the rate of school-associated violent deaths for male students was more than twice as high as the rate for female students *(Center for Disease Control and Prevention and U.S. Departments of Education and Justice – reported in The Journal of the American Medical Association, 2001.)*

Girls who bully are more likely to target their victim's feelings of social acceptance. Girls terrorize each other with covert campaigns of rumors which have become known as "relational aggression." Psychologist Charisse Nixon of the "Ophelia Project," has conducted two studies on relational aggression. She found that girls who are relational aggressive, tend to believe that this aggression is okay. The girls believe that if someone talks about them, it is okay for them to exclude them from the lunch table. Nixon reports that relational aggression can result in students changing schools, dropping out or even committing suicide. Long-term consequences can include depression, anxiety, academic and social problems, drug abuse and poor self-esteem.

Girls are more likely to form cliques or exclusive groups of "cool kids" and use this power to put others down. Those inside the circle cultivate an air of privilege and exclusivity and make themselves feel good by making others feel unaccepted and not good enough. Girls submit to the abuse of the clique so they will not be excluded. Boy's cliques are more often based on athletic ability than popularity.

BULLIES AS ADULTS

When bullies don't learn more appropriate ways of dealing with their frustrations and need for power, they continue to have difficulties as adults. Female bullies have more out of marriage pregnancies, lose more jobs, have fewer friends, become less popular throughout school and have more health problems (British Medical Journal, 1999.) A 1993 Norwegian study found that 60% of boys in grades six through nine, who were identified by both teachers and classmates as bullies were convicted of at least one crime by age twenty-four. The study reported, as many as 35% to 40% of male bullies had three or more convictions by age twenty-four, compared with only 10% of the total male population and 5% of the general population. Anti-bullying programs are much cheaper than the cost of incarceration.

Schools are not doing bullies a favor by allowing them to continue their destructive behaviors. Adult bullies are more likely to lose their job, have difficulties with the law, multiple divorces, higher rates of alcoholism and drug addiction and therefore more health problems. Dr. Leonard Eron reports that adult bullies seldom achieve socially or in their careers because they lack arbitration and mediation skills. Many adult bullies become spouse and child abusers. The real tragedy behind bullies is that they become victims themselves.

WHAT CAN SCHOOLS DO?

What can educators do with these bullies who often enjoy inflicting injury and suffering, lack compassion for their victims and feel justified in their actions? We must give up our desire for retribution, vengeance, punishments and stiffer sentences. When the main goal is payback to the bully for what they have done and make an example for others, hate and bitterness find rich soil in which to grow. Bullies do not change with spanking or traditional counseling. How bullies are treated in the schools will influence what kind of people they will become and what kind of lives they will live. Bullies must be deprogrammed and taught that bullying is a poor decision. This is a long difficult process. The goal must be to heal and restore, rather than condemn and punish. We must give up vengeance and look instead to repairing people and relationships. We must offer bullies more than to just wait for their incarceration. **Scandinavian Psychologist Olweus** documented thousands of changed attitudes and high success when schools established a school wide climate that did not tolerate bullying. Bullies can learn to control the aggressive behavior and must be provided opportunities for more positive ways to gain attention and make useful contributions.

WHAT STRATEGIES CAN SCHOOLS USE?

There is no simple answer to the problem of bullying and there are many philosophical approaches that can be employed. While some schools prefer one strategy over another, a mixture of approaches is often the most effective. Each bully has their own reason for bullying and therefore no one approach is effective with all bullies. Whatever approaches your school chooses doing nothing should not be one of the options. Educators must intervene and do whatever is necessary to stop bullying behavior as soon as they become aware of it. If the first approach used is not effective, try another and keep trying until you are successful. **No matter what you do, never bully the bully.** You are the adult, set the example. Students will never behave better than the adults who supervise them.

THE MORALISTIC STRATEGY

With this approach, the school must establish a high moral standard for student behaviors. The moralistic approach requires students to accept and conform to the stated values of the school. The staff applies moral pressure on students to demonstrate acceptance for school standards. Most students have the moral development to respond to this plan. Students that come from homes where kindness is expected and problem solving is practiced, merely conform to the moral code of the school. Unfortunately many bullies lack the moral development and problem solving skills to conform to values of caring and concern for others. Setting high moral standards does nothing toward understanding the values and motives of the bully. The bully may outwardly acquiesce to the school values and bully in ways which are even harder to detect.

THE LEGALISTIC STRATEGY

Under the legalistic strategy, the school establishes a set of clear rules against bullying and identifies specific consequences. There is little moralizing but rules are strictly enforced without bias or prejudice. A clear message is sent to students regarding what is acceptable behavior between students and what is not. This is the basis for the zero tolerance approach to bullying and violence. The effectiveness of this plan depends on the efficiency of the school's surveillance plan. Research shows that most staff members are unaware of most of the bullying that takes place on campuses. Although this method appears to demonstrate fair treatment, schools can end up punishing students with no malicious intent when rules are unintentionally violated. It is also hard to identify rules for all the behaviors that need to be addressed. Many of the favorite bullying techniques of girls such as isolation and ignoring display no overt actions. While penalties may deter some bullies, they seldom make much of an impact on the hard core bullies who can be encouraged by the threat of punishment. Zero tolerance rarely leads to any long-term solution because it does not address the causes of bullying nor does it teach any skills. At best, relying on rules and consequences, teaches students what not to do.

THE HUMANISTIC STRATEGY

When using this strategy, the school approaches the bully with the sincere desire to understand the bully and his/her needs. School officials listen to the bully, avoid preaching or laying down the law and engage in authentic two-way communication. The bully is treated with respect and an effort is made to identify the problem and seek a long-term resolution. The bully is given a chance to change his/her behavior rather than simply comply with the rules. For this strategy to be successful, the bully must be motivated to change. Bringing about change is very difficult and many bullies are very manipulative and good at pretending to alter their behaviors.

THE COMBINED STRATEGY

As was stated earlier, there is no simple solution. Even though preaching and moralizing will not abate bullying, schools must establish and uphold a high moral standard. Schools must establish clear rules and non-violent consequences, but they also have to acknowledge that rules and punishments are not really adequate. Corporal punishment often causes students to be angrier and more bent on revenge. Listening to bullies is not easy and takes more time. It is granted that schools must protect the victim, even if they can't convert the bullies. There continues to be many people who want nothing more than to extract revenge against the bullies. There are many strategies that can be used with awesome success. Finding the right strategy takes time and patience. Schools must decide that bullies are worth the effort.

METHOD OF SHARED CONCERN

In the 1990's, when I began looking for strategies to use in the middle school where I worked, I was not able to find research or strategies developed in the U.S. Fortunately people like **Alan Jenkins** from Australia, **Barbara Maines** and **George Robinson** in England and **Anatol Pikas** in Sweden had been developing programs and conducting research. *The Method of Shared Concern* is a program developed by **Anatol Pikas** (1989) and is the only model I found that is targeted specifically at bullying problems. Accusations are not made and blame is not leveled at anyone. **Pikas** also intended that both bullies and victims learn new skills. His plan does not include strategies for bystanders.

I used **Pikas'** model many times with students and found it very effective. I have outlined the plan as it was developed by **Pikas** but everyone knows that most educators adapt plans to their specific needs. I often did not follow through, nor feel it necessary to go through, all four stages of the plan. I use what I call "The Law of Least Intervention" which means, I do the smallest amount necessary to get the results I wanted. Many times stage one and two were all I needed to address the problem. I am sure you will adapt the plan to your needs also.

Stage One

A short (five or ten minutes) individual interview is held with the bully. When the bully is seen individually he/she is more likely to act in a responsible way. The bully is interviewed first, so the victim cannot be blamed for informing. In the interview you:

- Establish rapport with the bully and listen without moralizing;
- Make no accusation or place blame;
- Express a sincere desire to understand the needs of the bully;
- Treat the bully as a person worthy of respect;
- Create a sincere desire by the bully to understand and appreciate the needs of others;
- Help the bully understand how the other person feels;
- Ask the bully for suggestions (What do you think will help?);
- Agree on a plan of action;
- Agree on another time to check on progress.

Stage Two

After the bully has been seen individually, the victim is interviewed. The staff member should determine if the victim's behaviors contributed to the problem. While the victim is never blamed for the bullying, he/she may need to learn skills to avoid future problems. Listen to the victim=s story and:

- Provide support and identify the victim=s needs;
- Determine if there were any provoking behaviors;
- Ask for suggestions of how to improve the situation;
- Be willing to offers suggestions if appropriate;
- Agree upon a plan of action;
- Agree on another time to check on progress.

Stage Three

You will need to prepare for a joint meeting with the victim and the bully. If the bullying has ended, the meeting will be a final resolution. When preparing for the meeting:

- See the individuals again;
- Evaluate the success of the plan;
- Plan for a group meeting with the bully (bullies) and victim (victims), if the bullying has ended;
- Gain an agreement with the bully (bullies) that all comments about the victim (victims) will be positive and encouraging.

Stage Four

Hold a joint meeting with the victim (victims) and bully (bullies). The bully and the victim will make a public commitment of how they will act in the future. In the meeting:

- An adult should mediate to ensure that the students maintain order and the victim is protected;
- The responsibility for the solution is with the students;
- You should gain an agreement as to how the victim and bully will behave in the future;
- Identify what each party will do if there is a problem in the future;
- Put the agreement in writing if you feel there is a need.

STRATEGIES TO HELP BULLIES

Because every bully is different, there is no specific strategy that is appropriate for everyone. When there is an effort to understand the motives behind the bullying, you are better able to identify specific interventions that need to be tried. If one intervention does not produce the results you want, continue with another intervention. I do not address punishments as an intervention in this book. Schools have a lot of experience in the use of punishment, which at best teaches the bully what not to do. I am not suggesting that punishment be abandoned altogether, but I have identified some positive interventions that can help the bully learn skills they may be lacking and allow the bully to be given an opportunity to re-write their negative script.

1. **Some students bully because they have not learned to control their behavior. These bullies need to be taught self-control.**

   - Use Time for Self to allow the bully time to cool down. (Activity 5.1)
   - Provide instruction on relaxation strategies. (Activities 5.2 Learn to Relax, 6.10 Relax & 6.11 Relax and Move)
   - Teach self-monitoring skills. (Activity 5.3 Self Monitoring)
   - Have the bully participate in conflict resolution and/or anger management classes. (Activities 4.15 Conflicts Have Two Sides & 4.16 Mediation Works)
   - Instruct the bully in friendship skills. (Activities 2.4 Breaking Down Fears, 2.5 Meet My New Best Friend, 2.6 Just Like Me, 2.7 Appreciation Time & 4.13 Let's Be Friends.)

2. **Bullies often blame others for their behavior. These bullies need to recognize their behaviors are inappropriate and take responsibility for them.**

   - Bullies need to look critically at their behaviors and recognize behavior that is inappropriate. (Activities 5.3 Self Monitoring, 5.4 Attitudes About Bullying & 5.5 You May Be a Bully If…)
   - Bullies need to be required to repair or replace any items they have destroyed or damaged:
     If they wrote graffiti, they need to clean it up or paint over it;
     If they destroyed another person's property, they need to replace it;
     If they knocked down books they need to pick them up.

The parents of the bullies should be encouraged not to "bail out" their children. If the bully does not have money to provide restitution, they should be required to work to pay for their error. If parents can not find suitable work for the bully to earn money to pay for damages, the school should try to identify appropriate work for the bully. Parents could offer the bully's personal property to replace items they may have damaged or destroyed or sell their child's property to raise money for restitution. Bullies need to learn to face the consequences of their behavior. (Unit Three)

   - Bullies may need to write or make a sincere verbal apology to their victim to foster reconciliation. Make sure the bully has developed some remorse and do not put the victim in the position of being further embarrassed by a mocking apology. (Activity 6.7 Sticks and Stones)

- If the victim is willing, bullies could be asked to provide helpful services to compensate their victim for their bullying behavior. If they made rude comments, the bullies could make a positive comment. If everyone in the class heard the rude comments, the class should hear the positive comments. The bullies could carry books, clean out lockers, or provide other constructive task for their victim. None of these acts should be used to humiliate or penalize the bully but be seen as an opportunity for reconciliation.
- The bully could be asked to sign a contract and make a commitment to correct their behavior in the future. (Unit Two – Student Behavior Contracts)

3. **Because many bullies have troubled backgrounds, they may need counseling to help them deal with their personal difficulties and facilitate fostering empathy for their victim.**

- Individual counseling of students identified as bullies may be needed. Bullying can reflect abuse at home. An effort should be made to join with the student against the problem. When the student identifies why he/she bullies, then he/she can learn to develop better coping skills. (Activities 5.7 Why Do I Bully? & 5.8 Thoughts to Increase Self-Esteem)
- Help the bully identify his/her illogical thoughts and learn to think differently and act differently. (Activities 5.10 Rational and Irrational Thoughts, 5.11 What to Do Instead & 5.12 I Can Be Strong.)
- Use reverse role playing to help the bully develop empathy for his/her victim. (Activities 4.11 How Would You Feel? & 5.13 Who Is the Bully Now?)

4. **The bully needs to be provided opportunities to gain attention for more positive contributions. Positive activities can help the bully "re-write their negative script" and create an alternative, healthier role that does not involve bullying.**

- Help the students identify and develop their own interest and provide opportunities during or after school for students to make positive contributions. (Unit One – Opportunities for Community Service, Activity 4.6 I Can Help)
- Have the bully explore non-violence and write a report on a Nobel Peace Prize winner and present it to the class. (Activity 4.18)
- Teach students to complement others and act with kindness. (Activities 2.7 Appreciation Time & 5.15 Let's Be Kind)

TIME FOR SELF
Activity 5.1

Purpose
To help students learn to use self-control

Materials
Student Handout - *Time for Self*

Procedure
Ask the students:

- Have you ever had to have a "time out?"
- What did you do in "time out?"

Explain that when a teacher or parent puts you in "time out," they want to give you a chance to stop your behavior and think about your situation. There are times when your emotions "hi-jack" your brain and you end up in trouble because you reacted without thinking.

"Time for Self" is like "time-out," except that you are in charge. When you feel yourself getting angry or overly upset learn to take some ***"Time for Self."***

Give students the handout and review the steps with the students.

Follow-up
Ask the students:

- How will you know when you need ***"Time for Self?"***
- What makes it important to calm down before going to the next step?
- What are some ways to calm down?
- Do you feel you can ask teachers, friends, etc. to allow you to take some ***"Time for Self?"***

TIME FOR SELF

S Stop, walk away and calm down.

E Evaluate the situation and examine what is happening.

L Look for options and develop a plan of action.

F Follow through on your plan and evaluate the results.

LEARN TO RELAX
Activity 5.2

Purpose
To teach skills in relaxing.

Materials
None

Procedure
Explain to the students that relaxing is a skill, and like all skills you must practice to become good. There are a lot of anger management techniques but one technique everyone agrees on is that you can not be angry and relaxed at the same time. If you can learn to relax, you can control your anger. Whey you are angry, it is difficult to make good decisions. When you start to feel angry and you are tempted to do something impulsive or aggressive, stop, and take ten slow deep breaths.

Tell the students that you want to practice this relaxation exercise. Instruct the students to get comfortable in their desk, or allow students to sit on the floor or move to a more comfortable chair if available. To practice the breathing technique, instruct the students to breathe in through their nose and out through their mouth. When they breathe in; their stomach should pull back toward their back bone and when they breathe out the stomach should extend out. Have the students practice breathing from their diaphragm. Now tell the students to close their eyes and follow your instructions. Say some or all of the following instructions during this exercise. You can continue from 3 to 10 minutes depending on your group.

Use the following phrases to help teach the students deep breathing. Tell the students:
   "Breathe in slowly through your nose (wait three seconds) good – now breathe out through
      your mouth (wait three seconds.)"
   "Pull your stomach in (three seconds) and now out (3 seconds)."
   "Concentrate on your breathing."
   "Concentrate on the slow steady feel of your breathing in then out."
   "Breathe in calm and breath out stress."
   "Feel yourself becoming more and more relaxed with every breath."

Tell the students to open their eyes and ask them how they feel. Everyone should be relaxed and calm. Remind them that deep breathing is one of the best ways to relax. You may want to practice the exercise with your group at every session.

Follow-up
Ask the students:
* What makes it important to practice relaxation skills?
* What makes it important to use relaxation skills before you let anger get out of hand?
* What happens to your breathing when you get angry?
* What makes deep breathing incompatible with anger?

SELF-MONITORING
Activity 5.3

Purpose
To make students aware of the violence and aggression in their lives.

Materials
Masking tape

Procedure
This is an activity you will be able to use with several different self-monitoring lessons.

Explain to the class that exposure to negative comments, aggression and violence can have a negative impact on our attitudes and feeling. Often we are not aware of all the negative experiences we are exposed to. We are going to conduct a little experiment to monitor the negative influences in our lives.

1. Ask the students to keep track of the positive and negative comments they hear during a day at school. They are to keep a record of all the comments they hear whether from students, teachers or other staff while they are in school. They must decide if the comment is positive or negative. The comments do not have to be directed toward them. They will begin monitoring the positive and negative comments when they enter school property (the school, school bus, etc.).

2. Ask the students to keep a record of the positive and negative comments they hear for a full day. Ask them to start their recording when they wake up and continue to monitor until they go to bed. They are to record any comments that they hear. The comments do not have to be directed toward them.

3. Exposure to violence on TV, video games, movies and comics can desensitize students to violence in their lives and have a negative impact on their behavior. Ask the students to keep track of the acts of violence they witness on TV or video games for one evening. Have the teacher decide whether students are to monitor all forms of violence or just physical violence.

First, have the students estimate the number of comments (acts of violence) they think they will hear (see). Have the students write their name and estimates on a paper to be turned in.

Provide the students masking tape to put around their wrist. Provide the students with two pieces of tape if they are monitoring positive and negative comments. Explain that they are to make a tally mark on the tape for each comment or behavior being monitored. If you are recording positive and negative comments, identify positive comments on the right wrist and negative comments on the left.

SELF-MONITORING
Activity 5.3 *(continued)*

Follow-up
Ask the students:
- How close was your estimate to the actual tally?
- Did the results of this activity surprise you? Explain.
- How can we bring more positive influences into our lives?
- How can we learn to better deal with the negative comments (violence) in our lives?

Option 1 and 2
- Where did you hear the most negative comments?
- Who did you hear the most negative comments from?
- Where did you hear the most positive comments?
- Who did you hear the most positive comments from?

Additional discussion for Option 2
- Did you hear more negative comments at school or after school?

Option 3
- What effect do you think media violence has on your life?

ATTITUDES ABOUT BULLYING
Activity 5.4

Purpose
To help students recognize their attitudes about bullying.

Materials
Student handout – **Attitudes About Bullying**

Procedure
Tell the students that we all have different thoughts and attitudes about bullying. Our attitudes are often based on our life experiences. Because we have different experiences, we also can have different attitudes. It is good to look at our attitudes as compared to others and learn some facts to see if our attitudes are accurate.

Give each student an **Attitudes About Bullying** handout. Instruct the student to complete the survey.

After the students have completed the survey, inform the students that according to research, the response to all the questions should have been "Disagree." Discuss the following information with the students.

1. While some teasing between people of equal power is not bullying, most teasing is hurtful to the person being teased.
2. Most victims report that bullying is a big deal to them and causes them to become angry, depressed and fearful.
3. Bullying is never the victim's fault. No one "ask for it." Most bullies tease people who are different in some way.
4. Returning hitting with more hitting, usually leads to more hitting and seldom settles the problem.
5. Everyone does not have to follow what is "acceptable to the group." Being different is not a reason to be bullied. It is okay for people to be different.
6. For every person that is made tough by bullying, there are thousands that suffer emotional wounds that can last a life time.
7. If we are caring people we should respond when we see bullying by intervening or getting an adult to help.
8. While some bullies may feel badly about their actions, most enjoy the power and attention they get from being a bully.
9. People who complain about bullies are standing up for their right not to be bullied. They are behaving more maturely than the bully.
10. If you fight with a bully, you might get hurt, plus you might get into trouble for fighting.

Follow-up
Ask the students:
* Did any of you have attitudes concerning bullying that did not agree with the facts?
* What makes you think you had those attitudes?
* Have any of your attitudes changed concerning bullying?

ATTITUDES ABOUT BULLYING

Read each statement and circle the response that best describes how you feel.

1. Most teasing is done in fun and does not hurt people.

    Agree   **Disagree**

2. Bullying is really no big deal.

    Agree   **Disagree**

3. Most people who are bullied bring it upon themselves.

    Agree   **Disagree**

4. It's okay to hit someone who hits you first.

    Agree   **Disagree**

5. Bullying helps teach people what is acceptable to the group.

    Agree   **Disagree**

6. Bullying helps make you tougher.

    Agree   **Disagree**

7. When you see someone being bullied, it is best to mind your own business.

    Agree   **Disagree**

8. Bullies usually feel bad about their actions.

    Agree   **Disagree**

9. People who tell the teacher about being bullied are just "cry babies."

    Agree   **Disagree**

10. The best way to deal with bullies is by fighting.

    Agree   **Disagree**

YOU MAY BE A BULLY IF...
Activity 5.5

Purpose
To help students examine their personal behaviors.

Materials
Student handout – *You May Be a Bully If...*

Procedure
Remind the students that bullying can take many forms (physical, verbal and emotional). Bullies use behaviors to intimidate and control their victims. Bullies also have an attitude that the feelings of others are just not important. Some bullies justify their behavior and do not think there is anything wrong with what they do.

Tell the students that today we are going to examine our own behaviors and attitudes. Give students the handout You May Be a Bully If... Ask students to complete the handout independently. Inform them that this evaluation is for self-evaluation only. They will not be asked to share their responses with the class and the handouts will not be taken up. Allow time for completion.

After students have all completed the handout, inform them that if they marked any of these responses, they have some bullying behaviors. Have the students go back over the form and put an "O" by any of the behaviors they checked, that they "Often" do. If they marked four or more of the responses as "Often," they are probably a bully.

As you review the behaviors on the handout ask the students how the victim would feel in each of the situations.

Follow-up
Ask the students:
* Did you recognize all these behaviors as bullying behaviors? Why/Why not?
* Did you notice that many of these statements referred to feelings of anger?
  What makes you think anger is related to bullying?

Challenge the students:
* Examine your checklist and select at least two of the behaviors that you do and make a decision to stop those behaviors now.

YOU MAY BE A BULLY IF...

Put a checkmark by any statement that is true about you even some of the time.

_____ I pick on people who are smaller than I am.

_____ I often tease people until they get upset.

_____ I laugh when other people make mistakes.

_____ I demand that other people do things my way.

_____ I take or destroy other people's belongings.

_____ I like it when other students think I am tough.

_____ I get angry a lot and stay angry for a long time.

_____ Most things make me angry.

_____ I blame other people for things that go wrong.

_____ I like to get revenge on people who hurt me.

_____ When I play a game or sport, I get angry if I don't win.

_____ I get angry when someone else is successful.

_____ I threaten to hit, kick, etc. other people when I am angry.

SIMON SAYS
Activity 5.6

Purpose
To help students accept responsibility for his/her behaviors.

Materials
None

Procedure
Bullies often blame others for their feelings or actions. Is it really possible for someone to make us do anything if we really don't want to? We all played a game as children called "Simon Says." In the game you could win if you did the things that the leader said. We are going to play "Simon Says" in reverse. In this game you will win if you don't follow the leader's directions. For example if "Simon Says," stand up, you must sit down, or if the leader says, no talking, you must talk. If you do what the leader says, you are out. Make sure the students understand. You serve as the first leader. Include instructions as "Simon Says":

- sit down;
- hop on two feet;
- make an angry face;
- stand on one foot;
- make a fist;
- say you're stupid.

Play the game. It will be confusing at first but the students should catch on quickly.

Follow-up
Ask the students:
- What was hard about the game?
- Are we accustomed to doing what other people say?
- Can anyone make you hit another person?
- Who is in control of your actions?
- Who is responsible for all your actions, good and bad?

WHY DO I BULLY?
Activity 5.7

Purpose
To help students examine some of the underlying causes of bullying.

Materials
Student Handout - **Why Do I Bully?**
Paper, pencil and/or art supplies

Procedure
Distribute the handout **Why Do I Bully?** Lead the students in discussing the information on the handout. The information listed below can be used to enhance your discussion with the students. When discussing, be sensitive to the student's personal issues and experiences. Allow any student to pass when discussing the issues addressed in this activity if it is too personal or painful. Caution students not to mention the names of people when discussing specific situations. Offer to provide individual counseling on any of these issues at a later time.

Angry, Aggressive Families

Anger is normal and expected.
- Members of these families experience anger frequently and intensely.
- Anger and aggression is expected.
- Yelling and bullying behaviors seem normal.

Solve problems with anger and aggression.
- Aggression is misused.
- Bullying is considered a solution to problems.

No one listens until you get aggressive.
- Because family members argue, insult and threaten each other so often, no one listens to you until you get more and more aggressive.
- You become trained to listen only to anger.

Victims of Abuse or Bullying

Be very cautious when discussing abuse. You must discuss the limits of confidentiality with students. Tell them that you must report cases of abuse to the proper authorities. Point out that it is important to deal with the abuse before you can deal effectively with your relationship with others. Bullying and abuse should always be reported.

WHY DO I BULLY? *(continued)*

Feel Unhappy about Themselves

Some people with low self-esteem hate themselves and feel they never do anything right. Others are very sensitive, take everything personally and lash out at others when they feel hurt. Depression is high among bullies and victims, but suicide is higher among bullies. Having supportive friends lessens negative feelings.

Grief and Loss

Elizabeth Kubler-Ross, identifies anger as one of the normal stages in the grieving process. However, problems can arise when you stay in the anger stage and fail to work through the stages of grief and reach acceptance of your loss. People experience many losses in their lives and go through the grieving process. Loss and grieving does not have to be about death. You can experience the loss of a parent through divorce, imprisonment, abandonment and moving. The loss of friends, dating relationships, possessions and pets can also make you grieve.

Follow-up
Have the students complete one or more of these activities.
* Have the students write a story titled "Why I Bully."
* Have the students write a poem about their bullying.
* Have the students write about their feelings.
* Have the students draw a picture of bullying.

WHY DO I BULLY?

Bullies may come from angry, aggressive families.

Angry families teach the destructive habit of using anger to get their needs for power and control met. Bullies from angry families:

- Think anger is normal and expected;
- Try to solve their problems with anger and aggression;
- Believe that no one listens until they get aggressive.

Bullies may be the victims of abuse or bullying.

The National Institute of Child Health and Human Development's 2003 report revealed that 6% of students are both bullies and are also bullied. These students are at the highest risk for destructive behaviors. Victims become bullies when they:

- Don't know what to do with their rage toward their abuser;
- Direct their rage toward their abuser onto others;
- Try to make themself feel better by bullying others.

Bullies may feel unhappy about themselves and don't know how to make and keep friends.

Bullies with low self-esteem often feel:

- I'm no good;
- I have no friends;
- I don't belong;
- I don't even want to live;

Bullies may be suffering from grief or loss.

One of the stages in the grieving process is anger. Grief can cause people to be angry and respond negatively to others in their life. Bullies may be redirecting their anger from their loss to others in their life. Bullies blame:

- Anyone who has not had a loss or is not grieving like they are;
- Authority figures who did not prevent their loss or respond to their loss in appropriate ways (parents, teachers, or God.)

THOUGHTS TO INCREASE SELF-ESTEEM
Activity 5.8

Purpose
To learn to use positive thoughts to increase students self-esteem.

Materials
Chalkboard, chart or overhead.

Procedure
Explain to the students that bullying can have a negative effect on self-esteem. Some people with low self-esteem are really angry with themselves. They have set unrealistic expectations for themselves and therefore they fall short. These unrealistic expectations result in inflexible behavior toward others, demanding thoughts and behaviors, and negative emotions. People with low self-esteem often tell themselves these messages:

- I'm no good;
- I don't belong;
- I'm not loved or lovable;
- I have no friends;
- I'm not good enough;
- I shouldn't even be alive.

Unrealistic thoughts need to be challenged and changed. People can overcome low self-esteem by examining the thoughts they have and replacing them with positive affirming thoughts. Have students generate a list of positive thoughts and write them on the board or chart. Examples should include:

- I am important;
- I am a special person;
- I am lovable and capable;
- I am fun to be with.

Generate as many positive statements as you can. Go around the group having each student say a positive statement, about themselves to the rest of the group. Continue saying the positive statements until the students sound confident and everyone is in a good mood.

Follow-up
Ask the students:
- Did you have difficulty thinking of positive messages?
- Do you generally give yourself more positive or negative messages?
- How did it feel saying positive statements about yourself?
- What happens when we have negative thoughts about ourselves?
- Can anyone make you feel badly about yourself without your permission?

DEMANDS AND REQUEST
Activity 5.9

Purpose
To distinguish between demands and requests.

Materials
One deck of *"Demands and Requests Cards"* for every four students.

Procedure
Explain to the class that bullies often make demands and expect others to comply with these demands. When bullies make demands, there is often a spoken or unspoken "or else" built into the demand. Having people comply with their demands makes the bully feel powerful and in control. What bullies don't understand is that a "request" will often work as well as a "demand" and there does not have to be an implied "threat."

Define these terms for the students and discuss there meanings.
> **Demand -** A command that someone do something, an order.
> **Request -** To express a desire for.

For example, the statement "Give me a cookie," is a **demand**. "I would like a cookie," is a **request**. If a demand is not met, you must either lose face or make another demand. If you make a request, you should be prepared to accept either a "yes" or "no" answer.

Sometimes people do not realize how they sound when they are making demands. People are often more willing to comply with your wishes when you can "ask" for what you want instead of making demands.

Divide the students into groups of four. You can have the students go around the group saying "lions," and "tigers," and "bears," "oh my." Have the "lions" form a group, the "tigers," the "bears," and the "oh mys" form groups. Give each group a set of cards. Place the cards face down. In turn, each player selects a card, and states whether the message is a **demand** or **request**. If the player correctly identifies the card, the player keeps it. If the card is a **demand**, the student should restate as a request in order to keep it. The game continues until all cards are removed.

Follow-up
Ask the students:
* What made it difficult to distinguish between **demands** and **requests**?
* Which do you usually do, make more **demands** or **requests**?
* Would you rather others make **demands** or **request** to you?
* Can you accept it when others don't grant your **requests**, without anger?
* How can you cope when your **requests** are not granted?

DEMANDS AND REQUESTS CARDS

I have got to have
pizza tonight.

I am not going to bed
until this movie is over.

I would like to have
pizza tonight.

I would like to finish
watching the movie before
I go to bed.

You had better take me
to see that movie.

You had better call me
tonight or don't ever
call me again.

I would like to
see that movie.

Please try to
call me tonight.

You have got
to be my friend.

Give me that
paper now.

Your friendship is
important to me.

Please let me
see that paper.

RATIONAL AND IRRATIONAL THOUGHTS
Activity 5.10

Purpose
To help students identify their irrational thoughts.

Materials
Student handouts *Rational Statements & Irrational Statements*

Procedure
Explain to the students that bullies often have beliefs that are irrational or unrealistic. As long as your beliefs or expectations of the world are irrational, you will continue to experience unpleasant negative feelings such as anger, depression, panic, rage, self-pity and have a low frustration tolerance. These feelings can result in bullying behaviors and prevent you from having a good life.

When you realize that your thoughts are irrational and begin to think more rationally, you are better able to cope with difficulties, accept responsibility for your behavior and learn to treat others with respect.

Irrational Beliefs contain words and phrases such as:
- Awful;
- Terrible;
- Can't stand;
- Should/should not;
- Must/must not;
- Always/never;
- Absolutely.

(You may want to write these words on the board or a chart for the students to refer back to.) Tell the students that for each irrational thought there is a rational thought that can replace it. Give the students the following examples of rational and irrational thoughts. Have the students suggest other rational and irrational thoughts.

IRRATIONAL – Everyone should do what I want them to do.
RATIONAL – People will not always do what I want them to do.

IRRATIONAL – Everyone should be nice to me.
RATIONAL – I would like it if everyone was nice to me, but I know some people won't be.

IRRATIONAL – People always treat me unfairly.
RATIONAL – There are times that I may be treated unfairly, but there are times that I am treated fairly.

Divide the class into groups of four to six students. Give each group a set of rational and irrational belief statements. The statements are to be cut into sentence strips, mixed up and placed face down on the table or desk. Have group members take turns turning over a statement and stating whether the statement is rational or irrational. If the statement is irrational, they are to make a rational statement that could replace the irrational statement.

Follow-up
Ask the students:
* Why do irrational beliefs so often lead to anger and bullying?
* Do you recognize some of your irrational beliefs? Which ones?
* What kinds of feelings do rational feelings produce?
* Do rational beliefs help you overcome problems in your life? Why or why not?

Challenge the students to practice changing their irrational thoughts into more rational thoughts.

IRRATIONAL STATEMENTS

"It is terrible when things don't go my way."

"No one should call me names."

"You can't tell me what to do."

"You should not treat me in a way I don't want to be treated."

"I am always blamed for everything."

"Everyone should do what I say."

"It is terrible when you ignore me."

"I should get to do anything I want to do."

"It is awful when I have to do things that are difficult."

"Everyone should like me."

"I can't stand it when I am not in control."

RATIONAL STATEMENTS

"I don't like it when things don't go my way but I can stand it."

"I don't like being called names but I can't control other people."

"There are people who will tell me what to do."

"I cannot control how others treat me."

"There are times when I get blamed for things but not always."

"I cannot control what others do."

"I don't like being ignored but I can learn to deal with it."

"I don't like it when I can't do what I want but I know I can't always have my way."

"I don't like doing difficult things but everything can't be easy."

"I want everyone to like me but I know some people won't."

"I don't like not being in control but I can stand it."

WHAT TO DO INSTEAD
Activity 5.11

Purpose
To help students identify ways to respond to "pushes" with out "pushing back."

Materials
Student handout – **What To Do Instead**

Procedure
Ask for a volunteer to stand and face you. Encourage the volunteer to respond to your actions with whatever seems natural. Put your hands in the air as if challenging the volunteer to push against you. As he/she puts his/her hands against yours, begin to push against the volunteer. The volunteer should begin pushing back. Push harder and the volunteer will push harder. When it is evident to everyone that the two of you are pushing against each other, slowly stop pushing.

Ask the volunteer:
- What just happened?
- What happened when I pushed harder?
- What happened when I stopped pushing?

Ask the students:
- What are some ways students "push" each other? (You should identify typical bullying behaviors like teasing, name-calling, interfering with you, etc.)
- How do most students respond to these actions? (Respond back with more intensity.)

Hold up your hands again and ask the volunteer to push against your hands. When he/she pushes, do not offer any resistance and allow your hands to move back with their pushing.

Ask the volunteer:
- How does it feel to push without any resistance?
- Would you keep pushing if I did not offer any resistance? Why?

Tell the students that when someone "pushes" you, you do not have to "push back." There **cannot** be a struggle for power if you refuse to engage in their game. When you give in to your instincts and push back, the situation usually gets worse.

Give students the handout **What to do Instead** and discuss how students could use these suggestions when they feel they are being "pushed."

Follow-up
Ask the students:
- What makes it so hard not to "push back" when you feel you are being "pushed?"
- Which of these strategies do you feel you would be most likely to use? Why?
- Which of these strategies would you be least likely to use? Why?

WHAT TO DO INSTEAD

When someone is aggravating or interferes with you, you can choose to respond in ways that do not make matters worse. You can do one or more of the following things instead.

- Ask the person to stop the offending behavior.

- Tell the person how you feel in a firm calm voice.

- Walk away.

- Stop and think. Consider your options. Think about what might happen if you said or did something to make the matter worse.

- Remember that you are in charge of your actions and control your desire to act negatively.

- Tell yourself that it is okay to feel angry but it is not okay to hurt others.

- Breathe deeply in through your nose and out through your mouth.

- Look for an adult who might be able to help.

- Count slowly to "10." Keep counting until you feel your anger disappearing.

- Visualize yourself looking at the situation from above and see the behavior as silly.

- Think of something that makes you happy and smile.

- Treat the other person with kindness and respect. It is hard to be mean to someone who is being nice to you.

- Remember that getting back at someone never makes a conflict better. It only makes it worse.

- Find another person to be with.

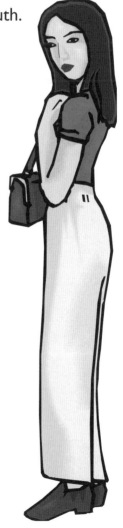

I CAN BE STRONG
Activity 5.12

Purpose
To understand the meaning of strength.

Materials
Copy of the quote.
I Can Be Strong handout.

Procedure
Write the quote from Dr. King on the board or present it on an overhead.

> ### *"The strong man is the man who can stand up for his rights and not hit back."*
>
> – *Dr. Martin Luther King Jr.*

Have a student read the quote aloud to the class. Lead a discussion of the quote and ask the class:
- What do you think Dr. King meant by this statement?
- Do you believe this statement is only true for a "man?"
- Based on this statement, does Dr. King feel it is okay to hit someone if they hit you first? Do you?

Give students the I Can Be Strong handout and review the instructions. Allow students time to write an individual response to each of the items. Discuss their responses to each situation and review with the follow-up questions.

Follow-up
Ask the students:
- Can you stand up for your rights without being violent?
- Is hurting someone's feelings a form of violence?
- Based on what we have learned, what do you think strength is?

I CAN BE STRONG

"The strong man is the man who can stand up for his rights and not hit back."
– Dr. Martin Luther King Jr.

Using Dr. King's quote as your inspiration, read each situation and identify the person who is being "strong" and tell why you feel they are being strong.

1. Frank calls Ralph a "chicken." Ralph replies "No I'm not" in a firm, calm voice.

   _____

   _____

2. Craig is teasing Terrie about wearing glasses. Terrie replies, "So?" in a questioning tone.

   _____

   _____

3. Dixon is threatening Michael. Austin walks over and encourages Dixon to leave Michael alone and go to class.

   _____

   _____

4. Matt comes up to Jeff in the hall and says, "I dare you to hit me." Jeff comments, "Matt I don't want to hit you, and I don't want to get in trouble."

   _____

   _____

5. Linda grabs Ann's purse and hold it away from her. Ann states. "Linda, please put my purse on the desk when you have finished looking at it."

   _____

   _____

WHO IS THE BULLY NOW?
Activity 5.13

Purpose
To help students develop empathy for the victim of bullying.

Materials
None

Procedure
Bullying has a negative impact on bullies and their victims. Victims often suffer humiliation, insecurity and loss of self-esteem. Bullies fail to cope with difficulties in their lives in appropriate ways and fail to develop empathy for others.

Define **Empathy** for your students as – The ability to understand how another person feels. Caution the students to not confuse empathy with sympathy which is feeling sorry for another person. Babies are born with empathy but life experiences can crush it out of a person. Developing your natural inclination toward empathy is what makes you capable of having caring relationships with parents, teachers, friends, and eventually your spouse and your children.

This activity is most effective when actual bullying episodes the students have either witnessed or participated in are used. If you are conducting this activity with students identified as bullies, have the students role-play specific bullying scenarios they have been involved in with the class. Caution the students that they are not to use names. In this activity, the student will role-play his/her victim and the teacher will role-play the bully. (Never allow students to role-play bullying, it will only reinforce that behavior.) Since you will be role-playing his/her behavior, have the bully describe exactly what he/she did and said. Ask the students to clarify by asking questions such as: "What made you say/do that," "What was your tone of voice, body language etc?" These questions will help you be more effective with your role-playing and will also cause the bully to examine his/her behavior and motives.

Conduct the role-play and allow it to continue until you feel the student can have empathy for the victim's point of view. If the student begins to get aggressive and lose control, stop the role-play immediately.

After each role-play, ask the student playing the victim the following questions:
- Describe how you would have felt if this had happened to you. (It is important to identify feelings. If the bully can't identify feelings, ask others in the group to supply words.)
- Is this how you wanted your victim to feel?
- Why did you want to make him/her feel this way?
- What was your goal?
- Did you reach your goal?
- Is there another way you could have reached your goal? (Encourage others in the class to help with suggestions.)

Role-play with as many students as you can.

Follow-up

Ask the class:

- Have you ever been embarrassed, humiliated and/or mistreated by anyone?
  How did it make you feel?
- Does making other people feel bad really make you feel better? Why do you do it?

Read this to your students and discuss it so your students will respond appropriately.

Frank Peretti wrote in his book *The Wounded Spirit*,

> Many of us adults have been carrying unhealed wounds since we were children. At the time of this writing, I'm close to fifty years of age, but I still remember the names and can see the faces of those individuals who made my life a living hell, day after day after day, during my childhood. I remember their words, their taunts, their blows, their spittle, and their humiliations. As I review my life, I think of all the decisions I shied from, all the risks I dared not take, all the questions I never asked, all the relationships I didn't pursue, simply because I didn't want to be hurt again.

I CAN HELP
Activity 5.14

Purpose
To help students develop a new identity.

Materials
None

Procedure
This activity can be used with one student or a group of students who need opportunities to make positive contributions. There must be a conscious effort to make sure that none of these activities are seen as punitive or retaliatory. Students should feel needed and appreciated for the work they do. The goal is to have the student make a positive contribution that they can be proud of and feel valued by others in the school community. It is critical that the student be **supervised** by an adult who is prepared to not only supervise but mentor, encourage, praise and build a caring relationship with the student. (Refer to Unit Two – The Teacher as the Model, Building a Relationship with Your Students, Discipline With Respect, Personal Student Conferences, I Refuse to Be Your Enemy.) The student's interest and talents should be considered when identifying service opportunities. Be sure to invest the needed amount of time in training the student to assure success.

Bullies often have negative relationships with their teachers, parents and others in authority. They feel trapped in negative roles and negative relationships. Victims of bullying feel isolated and caught in a cycle of ill-treatment. Both the bully and the victim benefit when given an opportunity to make positive contributions and perform tasks that are seen as important by their peers.

Students can participate in:
- Working in the school office – running of papers, filing, collating, etc.;
- Assist the school counselor – cleaning, assisting with guidance lessons, etc.;
- Assist in the lunchroom – unloading foods, washing dishes, cleaning, etc.;
- Tutor younger students – assisting students who are behind in skills and serving as a mentor and encourager themselves;
- Read to younger students – Students will practice their skills and give the teacher time to work with other students;
- Teacher's assistant – stapling, collating, cleaning, etc.;
- Helping the janitor – empting trash cans, cleaning, repairing, etc.;
- Designing and putting up bulletin boards – students who have artistic abilities could really contribute here;
- Teach skills to other students – identify any skill the student has (art, drama, golf, foreign language, singing, etc.) and let the students teach those skills;
- Assisting with special education or handicapped students;
- Aid for physical education classes – teaching skills, gathering equipment, cleaning, etc.;
- Assisting with after-school programs.

Follow-up
Monitor the student success on a regular basis. Provide positive reinforcement and encouragement as the student experiences success.

LET'S BE KIND
Activities 5.15

Purpose
Encourage students to be kind.

Materials
None

Procedure
This activity can be used with one student, a group or an entire class. Discuss with the students what constitutes an act of kindness (helping, complementing, encouraging, etc.) Ask specific questions such as:
- When someone drops his books, what would be the kind thing to do?
- When someone needs a pencil, what would be the kind thing to do?
- When someone gets a hair cut or is wearing something new, etc., what can you say?

Option one:
Identify a person to complement. It is often good to identify a teacher for the first time because teachers are more likely to respond to the complement appropriately. Discuss way to make complements, body language, tone of voice, etc.

Option two:
Encourage the students to be more conscious of opportunities to be kind and helpful. Ask the students to perform three (more or less depending on the students) acts of kindness in the next 24 hours (or before your group meets again.) The act can be identified or anonymous. Discourage the students from loaning money or personal property (pencils, paper, etc. would be okay).

Follow-up
After the students have performed their acts of kindness, ask the students:
- How did people respond to your complements or acts of kindness?
- How did this activity make you feel?
- Are there people who have a difficult time accepting complements (accepting acts of kindness)?
- How do you feel when people complement you (are kind to you)?
- If the student anonymously performed an act of kindness, ask how this made them feel?
- What would our school be like if everyone complemented more (looked for opportunities to be kind)?

Challenge the students to continue to look for opportunities to be kind and complement others on a regular basis. If you are meeting on a regular basis keep a record of the student's acts of kindness.

Unit Six
Helping the Victim – Skills for the Bullied

HELPING THE VICTIM:
SKILLS FOR THE BULLIED

**We cannot learn from one another
until we stop shouting at one another,
until we speak quietly enough
so that our words can be heard
as well as our voices.**

– Richard M. Nixon, U.S. President

**It is not what name others call you that matters,
But what name you respond to that truly
determines who you are.**

– Swahili Saying

HELPING THE VICTIM

Every day in every school in the United States, students are being bullied. In 2001, the *National Institute of Child Health and Human Development* reported that 1.6 million children in grades 6 through 10 are bullied at least once a week. A 2001 study by the *Kaiser Family Foundation* and *Nickelodean* reported that 74% of eight and eleven-year-old students said teasing and bullying occurred at their schools and 38% said threats of violence occurred. Schools can no longer throw up our hands and claim there is nothing they can do. Protecting the victim of bullying is the moral thing to do and schools have a moral obligation to protect the victims of this abuse. When teachers tolerate or show indifference to bullying, they are sending a subtle message to all their students that the teacher condones the bully's behavior.

At times adults blame the victims for being weak and not being able to stand up for themselves. Many students are bullied for things totally beyond their control. Looking different is often cited as one of the main reasons students are victimized. Personality type and speech were cited as causes of bullying more often than race or religion. Victims feel more afraid because they are usually warned by their bullies not to tell anyone. Returned aggression is not usually effective, and in fact can excite the bully into further attacks. Research by the *Bureau of Justice Statistics on School Crime* indicated that 80% of the time, an argument with a bully will end up in a physical fight. Assertion, rather than aggression, is effective however. Victims must feel safe in reporting bullying and must develop skills to deal with their bullies successfully.

Victims of bullying begin to dislike school. They do not trust their teachers or parents to protect them and they often develop depression, anxiety and low self-esteem (D. Olweus, *The Education Digest*, March, 1988). The *Office of Juvenile Justice and Delinquency Prevention's* 2001 research indicates that those who are bullied are at greatest risk of experiencing loneliness, trouble making friends, lack of success in school and problem behavior such as smoking and drinking. Victims often suffer from humiliation, insecurity and loss of self-esteem and they are at greater risk of suffering from depression and other mental health problems that can continue into adulthood. In rare cases, the victims of bullying commit suicide. A 1999 study by the *British Medical Journal* reports increased prevalence of depression and severe suicidal ideation among the victims of bullying. To some victims of bullying, death is better than facing the pain and persecution heaped on them every day by their tormentors.

While bullying often interferes with academic grades and the enjoyment of school, it can also turn a shy child into a loner and a sad child into an angry one. Being a victim of bullying can destroy the courage a student needs to raise his/her hand, try out for a sport or invite a friend to spend the night. Some victims of bullying develop a sense of hopelessness. About 10% of students who drop out of school nationally, do so because of repeated bullying (NEA.) Most victims carry emotional scars with them for the rest of their lives. Victims often feel they have no one to turn to and they can see no way out. Frank Peretti records in his book *The Wounded Spirit*, "I think of all the decisions I shied from, all the risks I dared not take, all the questions I never asked, all the relationships I didn't purse, simply because I didn't want to be hurt again."

The *Archives of Pediatric and Adolescent Medicine* reported that those who were bullied or were bullying were more likely to be involved in violent behavior. The report indicated that those who are bullied carry weapons because they might think they are in danger. The center for *Disease Control and Prevention* and *U.S. Departments of Education and Justice* reported findings in 2001 that indicated that homicide perpetrators were more than twice as likely as homicide victims to have been bullied by peers. While most victims of bullying don't take it to the point where they kill themselves or others, many will express visions of revenge and the desire to get even with their tormentors. Alfred University's 2001 study reported that 87% of teens said school shootings are motivated by a desire to "get back at those who have hurt them." *The Josephson Institute of Ethics* surveyed middle and high school students. The 2001 report showed that 39% of middle school students and 36% of high school students don't feel safe at school.

The victims of bullying can learn to speak up and report aggressive behavior and they will more often, when the school authorities take the charges seriously. Students can be taught assertiveness training to avoid victimization. Teachers, parents, counselors and other caring adults can help students gain self-esteem. Students support from other students, that are not typical victims, can be a major factor in turning victims around.

WHO ARE THESE STUDENTS AND WHY ARE THEY BULLIED?

Students who are bullied are often the students who:
- Are picked last for teams;
- Sit alone on the playground;
- Wonders why others don't like them;
- Are called hurtful names;
- Are socially withdrawn;
- Are treated as if they don't exist;
- Are largely ignored or rejected.
- Relate better to adults than other children.

Students are often bullied because:
- They are different in their appearance.
    - They are overweight or underweight, overly tall or short, etc.
    - They may be physically weak or disabled.
    - They have a less attractive facial appearance.
    - They don't have the "accepted" clothing.
    - They are often overly emotional and/or cry.
    - They have gender identity issues.

- They have deficits in the area of social status.
    - Their grades are too high or too low.
    - They have a low socioeconomic status.
    - They are members of a minority group.
    - They are not seen as being popular.
    - They are friends with another student who is bullied.

- They have physical, emotional or learning disabilities that can be manifested in inappropriate social behaviors. They may have conditions such as:
    - ADHD
    - Pervasive Developmental Disorders (Autism, Asperger's, etc.)
    - Sensory Integration Disorder

CONSEQUENCES OF BULLYING

Because most bullying is done under the "teacher radar," it is important for teachers to be more aware to the subtle messages students send that they may be being bullied. Students who are socially isolated and/or chronically bullied more likely to:

- Complain of headaches and/or stomach pain;

- Have excessive absences and/or check outs;

- Appear depressed;

- Seem fearful;

- Hold their anger just under the surface;

- Appear to be nervous;

- Cry or become upset easily;

- Seem to have low self-esteem;

- Be reluctant to participate in group projects or learning groups;

- Be physically weaker than their peers;

- Don't want to go to the lunchroom or have poor appetites;

- Request to go to the restroom during class rather than during times when the restroom may be crowded;

- Be underachievers and receive poor grades when they have the ability to make good grades;

- Withdrawal from activities they may have previously participated in;

- Have over-protective parents, and are overly close to parents.

193

TEACHER INTERVENTIONS FOR THE VICTIM

Teachers must intervene immediately when they are aware of bullying and stop the interaction without delay. Resist the desire to make a quick assessment of the incident and take time to talk to students who are involved.

- Have a serious talk with the victim as soon as possible after the bullying incident. Document the specific bullying episode and include how the bullying started, what happened, how it ended, who participated, and who witnessed it.

- Working cooperatively with the victim, determine a plan of action in dealing with the bully. Refer the victim to resources that are available. Reassure the victim that all possible steps will be taken to prevent a reoccurrence.

- Monitor the behavior of the bully and the safety of the victim.

- If the bullying incident is determined to be serious or if the bullying has become chronic, the teacher should contact the parents of the students involved. If a meeting is necessary, there should usually be a separate meeting with each family. A teacher might want to invite the school psychologist, guidance counselor, or principal to attend this meeting.

- There should be follow-up communication with the students, parents and with other teachers and administrators regarding the situation, until it is clearly resolved. Copies of all reports should be sent to the parents of the students involved and placed in the students' discipline files.

- If an anti-bullying plan is in place and the problem persists despite these measures, the aggressive student should be moved to another classroom or an alternative program (consult your school's policies). This solution should not be rushed into or immediately considered. Moving a bully into another program should be a result of careful consideration and only after parents and teachers are consulted.

STRATEGIES TO HELP THE VICTIMS

1. Present the students with **education on bullying** and its consequences. (Activities 2.1 *What Is Bullying?*, 2.2 *Styles of Bullying*, 4.1 *Let's Discuss Bullying*, 4.2 *Bullying Is About Power*, 4.3 *Write About Bullying*, 4.4 *Read About Bullying* & 6.1 *Bullying Inventory*)

2. Help the student **feel a part of the class** and assist in increasing communication and bonding within the classroom. This is especially important for students who are shy and reserved and those with disabilities. (Activities 2.4 *Breaking Down Fears*, 2.5 *Meet My New Best Friend*, 2.6 *Just Like Me* & 2.7 *Appreciation Time*.)

3. Provide **assertiveness training**. Most victims of bullying look like victims. These students need to learn to maintain eye contact and stand speak and walk assertively.

   - Make students aware of policies concerning reporting bullying behaviors and instruct them on how to report bullying incidents. (Unit One – *Reporting Bullying Behavior*.)

   - Teach students to look assertive. (Activity 6.2 *Being Assertive Helps*)

   - Teach students to speak assertively. (Activity 6.3 *The "I Messages" Have It*)

   - Instruct students on safety skills. (Activities 6.4 *Think Safety First* & 6.5 *Be Safe Going To and From School*)

   - Encourage the parents to have their child participate in private self-defense classes.

4. Help victims deal more effectively with their negative **feelings**. Victims of bullying often harbor feelings of anger, frustration, humiliation and rage. If these students are not able to effectively deal with their feelings, they can erupt into violent behaviors, drop out of school and/or carry these negative feelings into their adult lives and relationships.

   - Help students identify and change behaviors and thoughts that are having a negative impact on their self-esteem. (Activity 6.6 *Changing Self-Defeating Behaviors*)

   - Present instruction on dealing with negative feelings. (Activities 6.7 *Sticks and Stones*, 6.8 *My Feelings Are Important* & 6.9 *It's Not Fair*)

   - Train students in relaxation techniques and positive visualizations. (Activities 5.2 *Learn to Relax*, 6.10 *Relax* & 6.11 *Relax and More*)

5. Provide opportunities for **social skills training**. Often victims who have been mistreated are withdrawn and afraid of social interactions. Students who are shy and reserved and those with certain disabilities have limited social skills. These students often profit from social interactions and skill building with other students in settings where they may be less afraid to open up and show some leadership.

- Provide instruction on mediation. (Activity 4.16 *Mediation Works*)

- Offer opportunities to learn problem solving skills. (Activity 4.15 *Conflicts Have Two Sides*)

- Conduct classes on friendship. (Activities 4.13 *Lets Be Friends*, 6.12 *Enemies or Friends*, 6.13 *Making Friends* & 6.14 *Treating Others With Respect*)

- Provide instruction on response skills and opportunities for practice. (Activities 6.15 *Ignore*, 6.16 *Agree or Disagree*, 6.17 *I'm Not Purple*, 6.18 *I'm Neutral*, 6.19 *Don't Push Back*, 6.20 *Ask Them to Stop*, 6.21 *I'm Confused*, 6.22 *Use Humor*, 6.23 *Ask Questions*, 6.24 *Did That Make Sense?*, 6.25 *I'm Concerned About You* & 6.26 *Complement the Bully*)

- Provide opportunities for individual and group counseling. Group interaction is a great place for students who are bullied to practice new social skills and build a support group.

6. Help the students **build on their strengths and identify weaknesses.** All students have gifts and talents. Sometimes these talents are not as widely valued by their peers as athletic abilities but they may be highly valued in the adult world. Encourage parents to help by providing private instruction to build their child's skills.

- Provide opportunities for all gifts and talents to be recognized and encouraged. When the school offers a variety of extra-curricular activities for a variety of gifts and talents there is more of a sense of belonging and friendships among the students. Victims of bullying may have one place within the school where they feel they are accepted.

- Teachers and the administration need to recognize and value all talents. The students are more likely to value diverse talents if the staff does.

- Provide leadership opportunities for students where they can demonstrate their strengths. Students can tutor, serve as a teaching assistant, help with computer problems and provide numerous services to the teachers and staff. There are many ways that artistic, musical, writing, academic and organizational skills can be an asset to the school at large.

- Encourage positive relationships with adults. Students who are bullied need an adult within the school whom they can go to for help and support. This relationship needs to be more a mentoring relationship rather than a "teacher's pet." Students who are bullied frequently need an adult who can offer protection, emotional support and assist with problem solving.

BULLYING INVENTORY
Activity 6.1

Purpose
To help students identify the type(s) of bullying they experience most.

Materials
Student handout – **Bullying Inventory**

Procedure
Tell the students that there are many types of bullying: verbal, physical, emotional and harassment. Whatever form bullying takes; it is disrespectful and hurtful. Knowing the type of bullying you are experiencing could help you decide how to respond to it. We are going to take a survey to determine the type of bullying that you are experiencing most often.

Have the students complete the **Bullying Inventory** individually. After students have completed the inventory, inform them that the first group of five represents verbal bullying, the next physical, the third group is emotional bullying and the last group is harassment. (If you do not want to deal with sexual or gender issues, white-out the last two items on the handout.)

Follow-up
Ask the students:
- Are you experiencing one main type of bullying or several?
- Does one type bother you more than another?
- How are you responding to the bullying now?
- How is that working for you?
- What are some skills you would like to learn in order to deal more effectively with the bullying you are experiencing?

BULLYING INVENTORY

Read each statement and put a checkmark if the statement has been true for you.

During the last month people have:

_____ called me names;

_____ teased me in a way I did not like;

_____ said rude and mean things about me;

_____ said things that were meant as a put-down;

_____ shouted at me;

_____ kick and/or hit me;

_____ threatened to beat me up;

_____ tried to scare me by making physical threats;

_____ took something away from me;

_____ intentionally tripped or bumped into me;

_____ wouldn't let me join their group;

_____ spread lies about me;

_____ made sure I wouldn't sit with them at lunch;

_____ encouraged others to leave me out;

_____ spread rumors about me on the Internet;

_____ was mean to me because I was of a different religion;

_____ threatened me to compel me to give them money;

_____ said rude things about my racial, ethnic or religious group;

_____ made sexual comments that made me feel uncomfortable;

_____ called me gay or fag.

BEING ASSERTIVE HELPS
Activity 6.2

Purpose
To help students learn to look assertive.

Materials
Student handout – *Being Assertive Helps*
Chalkboard, Chart or Overhead

Procedure
Most victims of bullying look like victims. Bullies have reported that they can pick a victim that will not fight back by looking at the impression they give. When people stand, walk and speak with confidence they are less likely to be the victims of bullying.

Ask the students to brainstorm ideas of how a person can look and sound assertive. Write the suggestion on the board, a chart or an overhead. After you have a good list on the board, give students the *Being Assertive Helps* handout. Tell the students that this acronym can help them remember how to be assertive.

Tell the students that being assertive takes confidence and practice. Ask for volunteers to practice being assertive using the **"HELPS"** acronym.

Present the following scenarios and have the volunteers practice responding assertively.

- Someone is standing in front of your locker and you need to get a book out.
- A student grabs a paper you are reading out of your hand.
- Someone in your learning group takes credit for work you did.
- A person is spreading rumors about you.
- The person in front of you in the lunch line is talking and the line has stopped. You want to get your food.
- Someone in your learning group is not doing their share of the project.

Follow-up
Ask the students:
- Are some people more naturally assertive than others?
- Can you all learn to be more assertive? How?
- What is the hardest thing about being more assertive?

Challenge the students:
- I want all of you to practice these assertiveness skills every day.
- Look for situations where you can practice your assertiveness skills.
- Practice standing tall and making eye contact.

Being Assertive "Helps"

H   **Hold your head high and stand up straight.**

E   **Eye contact gives you confidence.**

L   **Lean forward and speak with a firm voice.**

P   **Picture yourself solving the problem.**

S   **Speak up and respectfully make your needs known.**

THE "I Messages" HAVE IT
Activity 6.3

Purpose
To teach students to use "I Messages"

Materials
Student handout *The "I Messages" Have It*

Procedure
Explain to the students that one of the most direct ways to make our needs and feelings known is to ask for what we want. Remind the students that we not only communicate our needs with our words but also with our tone of voice and body language. It is important to communicate the same message with everything we say and do. When we ask for something with anger or frustration in our voice, people are more likely to respond to us with anger and may refuse our request. They are called "I Messages" because you are putting the focus on your feelings, wants and needs. "You" puts the other person on the defensive. (You make me mad, you better stop, etc.)

Give students the handout and review the process with the class. Have the students role-play using "I Messages" using the following scenarios. Ask for volunteers to respond.
- A classmate shouts an ethnic insult at you.
- Someone breaks in front of you in the cafeteria line.
- You feel your grade in science is incorrect.
- Your parents have not extended your curfew in over a year.

Follow-up
Ask the students:
- Will you always get what you want with "I Messages?"
- What is the hardest part of the 'I Message?"
- What makes it important to use a firm calm voice when using "I Messages?"

THE "I MESSAGES" HAVE IT

Always start with "I" and clearly say _how_ you feel.

"I feel _____"   Example: "I feel frustrated."

In a clear firm voice say _what_ the other person did (or is doing) that made you feel that way.

"When you _____"   Example: "When you call me names."

Explain _why_ you feel the way you do.

"Because _____"   Example: "Because that is not true."

Clarify _what_ you want or need the other person to do.

"I want you to _____"   Example: "I want you to stop calling me names."

Examples:

"I feel upset when you trip me because I dropped my books and I want you to pick my books up."

"I feel embarrassed when you make fun of my hair cut because people laugh and I want you to stop making those comments."

THINK SAFETY FIRST
Activity 6.4

Purpose
To help students recognize and evaluate dangerous people and situations.

Materials
Student handout – **Think Safety First**
Chalk board, chart or overhead

Procedure
Explain to the students that the most important thing to remember about bullies is that they can be dangerous. 80% of the time an argument with a bully will end up in a physical fight. Fighting is not an acceptable way of dealing with problems.

It is important to be able to evaluate a situation and determine your level of risk for violence. If you are concerned that a bully is about to become violent, it is important to have a plan to get out of the situation.

Ask the students to identify strategies to help you stay safe. List the suggestions on the board, chart or overhead and discuss the potential success of the suggestions.

Give each student the **Think Safety First** handout and review it with the class. You may want to have the students role-play violent facial expressions and body language. Make sure students know how to safely create a distraction or call attention to danger they may be in. Especially make sure the students know who to go to for help and how to make a report of violent bullying behaviors.

Follow-up
Ask the students:
- What is the most important thing you learned from this activity?
- Is leaving a potentially violent situation a cowardly thing to do? Why/why not?
- How can you make sure that your behaviors do not provoke a bully to become more aggressive?

THINK SAFETY FIRST

1. Immediately walk toward a friend and/or adult and get help if:

- You are alone;
- The bully has a weapon;
- The bully is under the influence of drugs and/or alcohol.

2. Stay away from bullies.

- Don't go to places where bullies hang out.
- Stay with your friends. Bullies are less likely to bother you when you are with others.
- Move closer to the teacher so the teacher can see what is happening and intervene.
- Have a nonverbal cue that will let the teacher know you need help with a bully.

3. Look for signs that the bully is becoming violent.

- Observe their facial expression and watch for aggressive body language.
- Notice when verbal bullying becomes threatening and violent in nature.
- Watch for efforts to block your movements.

4. Try strategies to divert the bully's attention.

- Call a teachers' name loudly even if the teacher is not there.
- Drop your books or make other noises to draw the attention of others.
- If there are bystanders, ask them to observe what is happening.

5. Know where to go for help. Don't be embarrassed, everyone needs help at times.

- Identify teachers or friends that you trust to ask for help.

BE SAFE GOING TO AND FROM SCHOOL
Activity 6.5

Purpose
To help students develop safety strategies for going to and from school.

Materials
Student handout – **Be Safe Going To and From School**
Chalk board, chart or overhead

Procedure
Going to and from school can be the most vulnerable times for students and bullying. Even if the school is not be legally responsible for their students once they leave the school grounds, bullying occurring when students go to and from school can impact what happens on the school grounds. Students should be encouraged to report to the school bullying incidents that occur when students are walking to and from school. If the incidents involve other students, the administration should assist with the resolution of the conflict.

You may want to determine the need for this activity by asking the students:
- Do many of you have problems with bullying going to and from school?
- What are some of the problems you are having?
  (List the problems students are having on the board, chart or overhead.)

If students are having problems and you have identified problems address these problems with the students. You can use problem solving strategies and/or use the student handout **Be Safe Going To and From School.**

Follow-up
Ask the students:
- When walking to and from school, what are some of the things in your environment that you need to be aware of?
- Other than the whistle or cell phone, what other ways could you let people know you need help?

BE SAFE GOING TO AND FROM SCHOOL

Here are some suggestions for staying safe going to and from school.

- Be aware of your surroundings at all times.

- Be alert to potential dangers and avoid locations that make you feel uncomfortable.

- Avoid certain routes or places where you think you may encounter problems.

- Walk with a friend or group of friends that you can trust.

- Carry a whistle to signal that you need help.

- If someone begins to bother you, change the route you take to and from school and/or the time you go. Vary the route and time from day to day.

- Identify businesses or homes along your route where you know you can go to ask for help.

- Carry a cell phone and call for help.

- Tell an adult what is happening and who is bullying you.

- If you have been physically attacked or have had serious threats of physical violence, a report to the police should be filed.

CHANGING SELF-DEFEATING BEHAVIORS
Activity 6.6

Purpose
To identify and challenge self-defeating behaviors.

Materials
Chalk board, overhead or chart.

Procedure
Tell the students that when people experience a lot of bullying or other abuse in their lives, they may turn to self-defeating behaviors in an attempt to deal with their negative experiences. Self-defeating behaviors such as eating too much, bulimia, drinking or blaming yourself for the bullying and abuse, works against you. Discuss with the students that many people continue to use self-defeating behaviors even though the behaviors are making the problem worse and creating new problems. Have the students brainstorm a list of self-defeating behaviors on the board, chart or overhead. The list should include the following: drinking, drug abuse, overeating, anorexia/bulimia, driving too fast, going along with things when you don't want to, violence, giving up and suicide.

As a group, brainstorm a list of alternatives to self-defeating behaviors and write them on the board. The list should include: talking to a friend, counselor or teacher, learning to relax, learning to think differently, going to a self-help group, being more assertive, etc.

If students have identified self-defeating behaviors, encourage them to set a goal of adopting healthier behaviors.

Follow-up
Ask the students:
- What are your self-defeating behaviors doing for you?
- What are the beliefs or thoughts behind your self-defeating behaviors?
- Will you be healthier if you give up your self-defeating behaviors?
- Have you ever eliminated any self-defeating behaviors before? How? What were the results?

STICKS AND STONES
Activity 6.7

Purpose
To help students the negative impact of cruel words

Materials
Paper and pencil

Procedure
Introduce the expression:
"Sticks and stones may break my bones, but words will never hurt me."
Ask the students:
- Have you ever heard this expression?
- What do you think it means?
- Do you agree with this expression?
- Have words ever hurt you?

Point out that while words cannot physically hurt you, they can hurt your feelings and make you feel badly about yourself.

Introduce this new expression:
"Sticks and stones will break our bones, but words will break our hearts."
by Robert Fulghum.
Ask the students:
- Have you ever heard this expression?
- What do you think it means?
- Do you agree with this expression?

One form of bullying is name-calling and using put downs. There are times when we can ignore the names and not be hurt but there are other times when our hearts are broken by the things people say.

Ask the students:
- Raise your hand if you have **never** called anyone a mean name. (If someone raises their hand ask them to think carefully. You have never called anyone stupid, ugly, etc.)
- If you don't like being called names, why did you call someone else a name?
- How do you think the person felt when you called him/her a name?

Instruct the students to think about one person specifically that they have called a name. Have the students get out paper and pencil and ask them to write a letter of apology to that person as an offer or gesture of friendship.

Follow-up
Ask the students:
- Which of the statements from the beginning of the lesson do you agree with the most?
- At times, have we all hurt others with our words?
- At times, have we all been hurt by the words of others?

Challenge your students.
- If you are sincerely sorry for words you have spoken, I am asking you to be brave and give (mail) the letter of apology you have written to the person you have hurt.
- If you are sincerely sorry for words you have spoken, make a commitment here and now to never again use words to hurt other people.
- Read the dedication page of this book to your students.

MY FEELINGS ARE IMPORTANT
Activity 6.8

Purpose
To help students identify and share their feeling concerning bullying.

Materials
Student handout – *My Feelings Are Important*

Procedure
Instruct the students that how you feel directly effects how you act. If you feel positive about yourself and feel safe, you are more likely to learn and be happy. If you have negative feelings and are bullied, you are more likely to withdraw from others and are less likely to learn.

When you identify your feelings in different situations, then you can develop strategies to help you feel more positive and self-confident. Distribute the student handout – *My Feelings Are Important*. Inform the students that they will not have to share any of their responses if they do not wish to. It is important to identify feelings they are having. Have students complete the activity.

Open the class for discussion concerning their feelings in each of the situations. As a group, try to identify strategies to have more positive feelings at school. Be sure to discuss the importance of reporting bullying and how to make a report.

Follow-up
Ask the students:
* Are all your feelings in school negative or only in certain situations?
* Where or when do you feel the most positive at school?
* Are your feelings having a negative impact on your learning?

MY FEELINGS ARE IMPORTANT

**Describe your feelings in each of the following situations.
Try to use as many feeling words as possible.**

When I am at school, I feel: _____

_____

When I am in my classroom, I feel: _____

_____

During recess/P.E. I feel: _____

_____

During lunch, I feel: _____

_____

Going to and from school, I feel: _____

_____

When bullies harass me, I feel: _____

_____

Answer the following questions.

How often do you spend recess and/or lunch alone? _____

When you were bullied, who did you tell? If you did not tell anyone, why didn't you?

_____

_____

Who tried to help you when you were being bullied? _____

_____

IT'S NOT FAIR!
Activity 6.9

Purpose
To accept that things will not always be "fair."

Materials
Paper and pencil.
Chalk board, overhead or chart.

Procedure
Start the activity by having the students make a list of at least ten things about their life they consider enjoyable or their favorite things about their life. They can list material possessions, relationships, or personal characteristics and talents.

Encourage students to add to their list by naming the additional items. If they have these things you are mentioning, have them add the item to their list. (Leave out any items that might not apply to your students or might embarrass a student if it were mentioned)

Do they: live in a home, have loving parent(s), have friends, have a pet, have enough food to eat, have their own room, have a television, have a computer, have video games, have a bed to sleep in, have talents (athletic, musical, artistic, etc.), have a telephone. Are they able to attend school and get an education, have trendy clothing, have a car or truck, have a bicycle or motorcycle, have a yard to play in, live in the United States, have a hobby, and participate in clubs or church? Are they healthy, physically strong and free from disease?

Each student should have a long list by now. Explain to the students that **"It's not fair"** for them to have so many advantages when in some countries a majority of the people live in poverty and have no chance to get a good education. **"It's not fair"** that while they are healthy, there are thousands of children who will never be healthy. **"It's not fair"** that while they have food and a bed to sleep in, there are millions of children who are homeless and hungry.

Point out that many aspects of life are unfair. Some unfairness is positive such as the list they made, and some unfairness is negative such as getting blamed for something they did not do or being bullied and abused. Acknowledge that some of them have some real problems in their life that are **"Not fair,"** but if they added them all up, they would probably have more positive unfairness than negative. If we are willing to accept the advantages in our life, we must also accept that all that happens to us is not going to be pleasant.

Follow-up
Ask the students:
- Have you ever thought that people in other countries feel it is unfair for people in the United States to have so many possessions and advantages?
- Would you want everything to be fair?
- Does this activity make you think differently about unfairness?
- Is there anyone who does not experience some negative unfairness?
- How can "Counting Your Blessings" help you deal with unfairness in your life?

RELAX
Activity 6.10

Purpose
To help students learn to use relaxation to deal with anger and stress.

Materials
None

Procedure
Relaxation is a technique you can use to let go of stress and anger from being bullied. When you have less stress and anger in your life, the comments and actions of others will not bother you as much and you will be able to think of ways to deal with their behavior more appropriately. The more you practice a skill the better you become. We are going to practice relaxation today. I want to encourage you to practice at home and use the techniques whenever you begin to feel stressed or angry.

Have all the students get as comfortable as they can. You might want to allow the students to sit or lay on the floor for this activity. Follow the script below.

First I want you to close your eyes and we are going to do some relaxation breathing. Inhale through your nose deeply, and then exhale through your mouth quietly. Slowly inhale deeply then let your breath out. As you are breathing, count silently to yourself - 1,001...1,002...1,003- allowing the air to gently escape and the exhalation to come to a natural pause. Then begin the next breath. (Allow time for the students to get calm and relaxed with the breathing, then continue.)

As you are breathing, I am going to make some statements. Say these statements in your mind after I have said them and continue your relaxation breathing.

To the teacher: I have included many positive validation statements. Select the ones that are the most appropriate for your group. Make each of these statements, repeat them as needed and allow time for the students to concentrate on them then move to the next statement. This activity can last for 5 to 20 minutes based on your needs and time constraints.

Positive Validation Statements

- I am worthy just the way I am.
- I deserve to be treated with respect.
- I am capable of healing my emotional wounds.
- I can calm myself no matter what is happening.
- I know that in every moment, I am free to decide what I will say and do.
- I am capable of making everything that happens to me strengthen me.
- My past is behind me, I can direct my future.
- I will let go of my doubts about myself.
- I know there is a reason everything happens.
- I am free to let go of my pain.
- I can learn from silence.
- My highest self can lift me above the things I am experiencing.
- I know I can always have peace in my life.
- I am strengthened as I learn to control my thoughts.
- I know the way to transform my life is through love.
- I will look for the good that lies within everything that happens.
- I am already whole and do not need anything else to be complete.
- I do not need to dominate anyone to feel good about myself.
- Today I will do all I can to help others.
- Today I will work for the good of all.

When you have finished, calmly tell the students to open their eyes.

Follow-up
Ask the students:
- Has this activity made you feel calm and relaxed?
- How did you feel about the positive validations I made?
- What was your favorite validation?
- How can you use this activity to help yourself feel calm and relaxed?

Challenge the students:
- Practice relaxation on a regular basis in your life.
- Select one or more of the validations to mentally focus on as you go through your day.
- Use these validations when you are upset, stressed or worried to help you feel more calm and in control.

RELAX WITH MOVEMENT
Activity 6.11

Purpose
To help students who have difficulty sitting still learn to relax.

Materials
None – Because this activity required students to sit on the floor, you may want to have mats or towels for students to sit on. *(this activity would be inappropriate for girls wearing dresses.)*

Procedure
Students with ADHD and some of the other developmental disorders have difficulty with relaxation techniques that require them to sit still. This relaxation technique is based on yoga which promotes relaxation and movement.

Tell the students that relaxation is an important technique for everyone to learn. When you become overly excited, you are more likely to act impulsively and do something that will cause problems. Learning to relax can help you be less impulsive and you will be more likely to think before you act.

To the teachers:
Read through the script and make sure you understand the instructions. Read the following script to the students allowing time for movements. You can repeat the movements as many times as you feel is appropriate. The first time you do this activity there will be some confusion concerning the instructions. The more you do this activity, the more effective it will be.

Say to the students:
Everyone stand, close your eyes and we are going to practice deep breathing. I want you to stand on your toes and breathe in deeply through your nose and then slowly lower your heels to the floor as you breathe out. (Repeat several times.)

Now I want you to bend forward at the waist and let your head and arms hang limply. Feel the stretch in the back of your legs as your head and arms are limp. Breathe deeply in through the nose and out through your mouth. Slowly bring your body back up.

Now I want everyone to sit on the floor with your legs crossed and your hands resting on each knee. (Wait for all students to get into position.)

I want you to lift your shoulders to your ears and breathe in through your nose. As you drop your shoulders breathe out through your mouth. (Repeat several times.)

Now I want you to drop your chin down on your chest and let it hang feeling the stretch on the back of your neck. Breathe in and out deeply. Now slowly roll your head over toward your right shoulder breathing in and out. Hold your head to the right, feeling the stretch in your neck. Slowly roll your head forward again and then to your left shoulder breathing in and out holding the stretch. (Repeat several times.)

Now take your right hand and place it on the floor behind your back. Place your left hand on your right knee and slowly twist your body toward the right. Feel the stretch and breathing deeply. Now put your left hand behind you. Keep your right hand on your left knee and twist your body to the left. Keep breathing deeply.

Next put your right arm and elbow on the floor and lift your left arm over your left ear and stretch your body to the right. Feel the stretch and breathe deeply. Now reverse this and stretch to the left. (Repeat several times.) Now bring your body back up straight.

Now put both arms in front of you and let your body bend forward. Let all the tension go and bend your body forward as far as you can. Breathe deeply. Slowly roll you body and arms to the right and stretch as far as you can. Now slowly roll your body forward and then to the right. You should feel the stretch in your left side. Slowly roll your body and arms forward again. Continue rolling your body to the left and stretch your arms and body to the left. Remember to keep breathing deeply. (Repeat as many times as you want.)

Now bring your body straight up again and breathe deeply. Breathe in through your nose and slowly out through your mouth. (Allow the students to sit and breathe for a few minutes.)

Now open your eyes.

Follow-up
Ask the students:
- Do you feel relaxed?
- Will learning to relax help you be able to think more clearly?
- What was the most helpful thing about this activity?
- How can you use what you have learned to help you relax at other times?

Challenge the students:

- Practice relaxation every day to teach your body to calm down and get ready for activities that require sitting and attending and help you deal with annoying behavior from others.

ENEMIES OR FRIENDS?
Activity 6.12

Purpose
To help students change their attitudes and feelings toward bullies.

Materials
Overheads or posters with Dr. King's quotes.

Procedure
Present the first quote by Dr. Martin Luther King Jr. to the class either on an overhead or make a poster that can be displayed in the classroom.

"Let no man pull you so low as to hate him."

Remind the students that Dr. King was a leader in the civil rights movement in the United States during the 1950' and 60's. He used non-violent protest to call attention to the injustice and racism and win the hearts and spirit of the people.

Ask the students:
- What do you think Dr. King meant by this statement?
- How does hate "pull you low?"
- Do you think bullies want you to hate them?
- How did Dr. King's use of non-violence model this statement?

Present the second quote by Dr. King to the class.

"Love is the only force capable of transforming an enemy into a friend."

Ask the students:
- How does Dr. King suggest we respond to our enemies?
- How do you usually feel toward your enemies?
- Is it possible to "love" someone who is bullying you?
- Why is it hard to continue to be mean to someone who is being nice to you?
- Does the fact that Dr. King was a minister, help explain why he asked us to love our enemies?

Divide the class into groups. Remind your students that bullying can be a cry for help and many bullies are very unhappy with themselves. Sometimes bullies are mean to other students because they feel no one likes them. Remind the students to use Dr. King's quotes as their inspiration, have each group make a list of ways students can change bullies into friends by responding to them in more positive ways.

Inform the groups of how much time they are being given. Have the groups share their suggestions.

Follow-up

Ask the students:

- According to Dr. King, what does hate do to us?
- According to Dr. King what can love do for us?
- How can refusing to hate a bully take away some of his power?
- How can you apply these words of Dr. King in your daily life?

As an additional activity, you could have students research and report on other people who used non-violence to deal with injustice. Here are some men and women who were peacemakers.

Susan B. Anthony

Joan Baez

Helen Caldicott

Jaques Cousteau

Medgar Evers

Mother Mary Jones

William Penn

Pablo Picasso

Gandi

Eleanor Roosevelt

Benjamin Spock

Harriet B. Stowe

Henry Thoreau

Harriet Tubman

Raoul Wallenberg

MAKING FRIENDS
Activity 6.13

Purpose
To help students make and keep friends.

Materials
Student handout- **Making Friends**

Procedure
Tell the students that one of the ways to avoid bullying is to stay with your friends. Bullies are less likely to bother you when you are with others. At times, bullies are like predators, they try to separate their prey from the flock and attack them individually. You can stay with your friends and not give the bully a chance to attack.

It is important to have friends. The more friends you have the less likely you are to be bullied. Divide the class into groups of four or five. Tell the students to think of a person they know who has a lot of friends. (Caution them not to use any names.) Instruct each group to list things these people do which probably are the reasons they have a lot of friends.

Bring the groups back together and make a list on the board of ways to have friends. Give students the **Making Friends** handout and discuss these suggestions with the students.

Follow-up
Ask the students:
* To become good at a skill, you must practice. How can you practice friendship skills?
* What is the most difficult thing about making friends?
* What is the most helpful thing you have learned today about making friends?

MAKING FRIENDS

Making friends will be easier if you can follow these suggestions.

- Smile and say "hi" to people. Don't always wait for someone else to make the first move.

- Broaden your ideas of what a friend looks like. All your friends do not have to be from the same race, ethnic groups or have all the same interest.

- Tell the truth about yourself and what you stand for. Don't pretend to be something you are not. Friends appreciate honesty with each other.

- Watch what you say. It is more important to be kind than brutally honest. Honesty should not have to hurt.

- Believe your friends when they tell you your behavior is beginning to irritate them.

- Look for nonverbal signs that your behavior is bothering others.

- Volunteer for activities you have an interest in. Join clubs and take classes in or out of school.

- Be a good listener to friends when they talk and ask questions. Show an interest in them and don't just talk about yourself.

- Don't just go to your friends when you have problems. Share your joys, too. No one likes to be around someone who is always complaining.

- Be a giver. Friendship is about give and take. Be sure to do your share.

- Recognize "friends" you can do without. There are people who will pretend to be your friend but are really "users." Look for friends you can depend on.

TREAT OTHERS WITH RESPECT
Activity 6.14

Purpose
To help students learn good friendship behaviors.

Materials
Student handout – **Treat Others With Respect**

Procedure
Explain to the students that bullying is about an abuse of power and the lack of respect for the dignity of others. Bullies seldom have good friends. If you want to make and keep good friends you need to treat everyone with respect, especially in what you say and do. If you treat others with respect, you are more likely to be treated with respect. Respect is demonstrated by what you say, what you do and how you sound. Sometimes we don't recognize certain behaviors as disrespectful.

Give the students the **Treat Others with Respect** handout and review the direction. Allow time for completion. Once the handout is completed, inform the students that all the odd responses represent disrespectful behaviors or actions and all the even numbers represent respectful responses.

Follow-up
Ask the students:
- How does disrespectful behavior hinder with our ability to have friends?
- When we are disrespectful to others, how do they often respond to us?
- Why do we continue disrespectful behaviors even when we know they are disrespectful?

Challenge the students:
- Look through your list and select two of the odd numbered responses that you have checked. Make a commitment now to remove those behaviors from you life as of now.
- Make a commitment to be respectful to others even if they are disrespectful to you.

TREAT OTHERS WITH RESPECT

Put a check by all the things that you do even once in a while.

_____ 1. Laugh at others.

_____ 2. Smile at others.

_____ 3. Roll your eyes.

_____ 4. Give people complements.

_____ 5. Criticize others.

_____ 6. Offer to help.

_____ 7. Make fun of others.

_____ 8. Ask questions about things that interest others.

_____ 9. Raise your voice.

_____10. Congratulate others on their achievements.

_____11. Ignore people when they are talking to you.

_____12. Respond with kindness when others are sad.

_____13. Act superior to others.

_____14. Be willing to share.

_____15. Call people names.

_____16. Show interest in what others are saying.

_____17. Make demands of others.

_____18. Keep yourself healthy and clean.

_____19. Put people down.

_____20. Display acts of kindness.

IGNORE
Activity 6.15

Purpose
To help students know when to ignore comments from bullies.

Materials
None

Procedure
Tell the students that one strategy to use with bullies is to ignore them. Assure the students that this is not the only strategy they will be learning but there are times when ignoring the bully is helpful.

Ask the students what does ignoring mean? (Make sure they realize that ignoring means not giving any indication that you heard the comment or noticed the action. You do not look at them or acknowledge them in any way. You may want to have students practice this behavior.)

Tell the students that it is best to ignore the bully if:
- You do not know the bully;
- The bully is capable of hurting you; or
- When the bullying is occurring for the first time.

Discuss with the students why it is best to ignore the bully in each of these situations identified above. Bullies bully to gain power and attention. Because ignoring the bully does not give him/her the reaction he/she wants, he/she might stop the bullying. Assure the students that they do not have to ignore every offensive or chronic bullying and they can always ask an adult for assistance.

Follow-up
Ask the students:
- Have you ever tried ignoring the bully? How did it work?
- How does ignoring take power away from the bully?
- What did you learn about ignoring from this lesson that will help you the next time you try this strategy?

AGREE OR DISAGREE
Activity 6.16

Purpose
To help students learn to agree or disagree with the bully.

Materials
Chalkboard, chart, or overhead

Procedure
Explain to the students that if part of what the bully says is true, you can agree with the part that is true. If you are tall, short, wear glasses, dropped something, etc. then agree with the bully. There is nothing wrong with wearing glasses or even having big ears. The bully wants to embarrass you and agreeing with the bully can take away his power to embarrass you. When you agree with the bully use a "matter of fact" tone and make comments like:

- "I know."
- "You're right about that."
- "My barber did get kind of carried away."
- "I was kind of clumsy."
- "You're right, basketball just isn't my game today."

(You may want to write these responses so students can refer to them.
Encourage students to add additional statements.)

If what the bully is saying is not true, then in a firm, calm voice disagree with the bully. When you disagree with the bully, you can make comments like:

- "No, I'm not."
- "That is just not true."
- "That isn't right."

(You may want to write these responses so students can refer to them.
Encourage students to add additional statements.)

AGREE OR DISAGREE
Activity 6.16 (continued)

Role-play with the students by making the following statements and have the students respond by agreeing or disagreeing. Remind the student to use a "matter of fact" tone. You can go through the group making a statement to each student and have him/her respond or allow students to raise their hand if they want to respond. After the students have practiced making one response, continue practicing the skill by having them make multiple responses. Skip any statements that would be unsuitable or too sensitive for your students or add statements that may be more appropriate.

- You're short – tall – skinny – fat – clumsy – stupid.
- You're a geek – nerd – egghead – retard – klutz – crybaby – slut.
- You wear glasses – braces – shoes from Wal-Mart – clothes from Good Will.
- You've got big feet – ears – teeth – nose.
- You look like a pig – baboon – beaver – moron.
- Your barber really scalped you.
- What happened to your hair?
- Did you sleep in that shirt?
- You can't even walk without falling down?
- How could you have missed that ball, it was right over the plate?

Tell the students that they should not continue using this or any other strategy if the bully is becoming violent. Remind students that they can always ask an adult for help.

Follow-up
Ask the students:
- Have you ever used this strategy with bullies? How did it work?
- How does this strategy take power away from the bully?
- When do you think this strategy will be the most helpful?

I'M NOT PURPLE
Activity 6.17

Purpose
To help students disagree with the bully.

Materials
None

Procedure
This activity can be used to reinforce the student's ability to disagree with the bully without becoming angry or embarrassed. While this analogy will help many students, there are students whose self-esteem is so fragile; they are not able to use this activity.

Identify a student in your group that has a reasonable amount of self-esteem. Say to the student:

"If I looked at you and said you're purple, would you believe me?"
(The student should respond "no.")

"Would you look at yourself to see if you had turned purple?"
(Again the student should respond that they would not need to do that.)

"If I said you are purple, would that make you angry or hurt?"
(Hopefully the student would respond "no.")

"What would you think about me if I said you are purple?"
(Students should respond that you don't know what you are talking about, you are crazy, etc.)

"Why wouldn't it make you angry if I said you were purple?"
(Help the students realize that it does not make them angry because they know it is not true.)

Explain to the class that if you know something is not true and a bully saying that to you, it doesn't have to make you angry. If someone says you are stupid, and you know it is not true, it doesn't have to make you angry either. Just because someone says something to you, doesn't make it true. If you know it is not true, just think to yourself – I am not purple – and don't get angry about the comment.

Follow-up
Ask the students:
- How can this analogy help you disagree with the comments bullies make without getting angry.
- How does this strategy take power away from the bully?
- What are some ways that you can use this strategy?

I'M NEUTRAL
Activity 6.18

Purpose
To help students learn to use neutral responses with bullies.

Materials
Chalkboard, chart or overhead

Procedure
Tell the students that another strategy to use with comments made by bullies is to make a "neutral response." By giving a "neutral response," you are not agreeing or disagreeing with the bully. When using "neutral responses" it is important to use a "matter of fact" tone. If you start to become emotional, the bully will be encouraged. Bullies often want to start an argument, when you make a "neutral response" you are not being drawn into their argument. When you give a "neutral response" you would say things like:

- "So."
- "Whatever."
- "You noticed."
- "You may be right."
- "You're entitled to your opinion."

- "And your point is?"
- "I'm sure that is the way you see it."
- "It's okay, you don't have to like me."
- "Thanks for sharing."
- "Let me know when you get over it."

(You may want to write these so students can refer to them.
Encourage students to add additional statements.)

Role-play with the students by making the following statements and have the students respond with a neutral response. Remind the students to use a "matter of fact" tone. You can go through the group making a statement to each student and have him/her respond or allow students to raise their hand if they want to respond. After the students have practiced making one response, continue practicing the skill by having them make multiple responses. Skip any statements that would be unsuitable or too sensitive for your students or add statement that may be more appropriate.

You're short – tall – skinny – fat – clumsy – stupid.
You're a geek – nerd – egghead – retard – klutz – crybaby – slut.
You wear glasses – braces – shoes from Wal-Mart – clothes from Good Will.
You've got big feet – ears – teeth – nose.
You look like a pig – baboon – beaver – moron.
Your barber really scalped you.
What happened to your hair?
Did you sleep in that shirt?
You can't even walk without falling down?
How could you have missed that ball, it was right over the plate?

Tell the students that they should not continue using this or any other strategy if the bully is becoming violent. Remind students that they can always ask an adult for help.

Follow-up
Ask the students:
- Have you ever tried this strategy with bullies? How did it work?
- How does this strategy take power away from the bully?
- In what situations will this strategy be the most helpful?

DON'T PUSH BACK
Activity 6.19

Purpose
To help students resist arguing with a bully.

Materials
None

Procedure
Ask for a volunteer to stand and face you. Encourage the volunteer to respond to your actions with whatever seems natural. Put your hands in the air, palm toward the volunteer as if challenging the volunteer to push against you. As he/she puts his/her hands against yours, begin to push against the volunteer. The volunteer should begin pushing back. Push harder and he/she will push harder. When it is evident to everyone that the two of your, are pushing against each other, slowly stop pushing. Take your hands down and motion for the volunteer to sit down.

Ask the volunteer:
- When I put my hands up why did you put your hands up too?
  (They should respond that this is a challenge.)
- When I started pushing what did you do? (Pushed back.)
- What happened when I pushed harder? (They pushed harder.)
- What happened when I stopped pushing? (They stopped pushing.)

Have the students form pairs and go through this activity to see how it feels. Next instruct the person with the shortest hair in each pair to offer no resistance when their partner pushes.

Ask the students:
- How did it feel when you were pushing against each other? (They were in a struggle for power.)
- To the person who pushed ask, "How did it feel when your partner didn't push back?"
  (There was no struggle for power.)
- Was there any point in continuing to push? (No, because there was no resistance.)
- To the person who offered no resistance ask, "Did you feel powerless when you did not
  push back against your partner?" (Most should say "No," in fact they were more in control.)

Follow-up
Ask the students:
- What is your natural response when someone pushes you?
- What usually happens then?
- How does this activity demonstrate what goes on with bullies when you give a "neutral response?"
- How does not pushing back (giving a "neutral response") take power away from the bully?
- What are some situations where you can use "neutral responses?"

ASK THEM TO STOP
Activity 6.20

Purpose
To help students be more assertive and ask for what they want.

Materials
Chalkboard, chart or overhead

Procedure
Explain to the students that another strategy to use with bullies is to ask them to stop the behavior that is bothering them. When asking bullies to stop a behavior, it is very important to use a firm, calm voice. If you are becoming emotional, they know their technique is working. This technique can be more powerful if you call the bully by name before making your request. Ex. "Susan, I want you to stop." When you are asking the bully to stop their actions or comments you may make statement such as:

- "Go away and stop bothering me."
- "I don't like what you are saying to me."
- "I want you to stop saying (doing) that."
- "What you are doing is wrong (mean), stop."
- "I want you to leave me alone."
- "Name calling isn't nice, I want you to stop."
- "Why are you being mean to me? I have never hurt you?"
- "I'm asking you to stop."
- "If you don't stop, I'm going to get help."
- "I don't want to fight. Can't we be friends instead?"
- "I won't fight you because it's wrong to fight."

(You may want to write these statements so students can refer to them.
Encourage students to add additional statements.)

You may want to use what is called the "broken record" technique. This is where you continue to make the same request over and over. You would say:

- "Leave me alone, leave me alone, leave me alone, etc."
- "I want you to stop, I want you to stop, I want you to stop, etc."

Role-play with the students by making the following statements and have the students respond by making a statement asking for what they want. Tell the students that when using this strategy, you do not respond at all to the comments of the bully but continue to make your request. This technique can also be helpful when you are in the classroom or hallway because it can draw the attention of the teacher or others who might assist you. Remind the students to use a firm, calm voice. You can go through the group making a statement to each student and having him/her respond or allow students to raise their hand if they want to respond. After the students have practiced making one response, continue practicing the skill by having them make multiple responses. Skip any statements that would be unsuitable or too sensitive for your students or add statements that may be more appropriate.

- You're short – tall – skinny – fat – clumsy – stupid.
- You're a geek – nerd – egghead – retard – klutz – crybaby – slut.
- You wear glasses – braces – shoes from Wal-Mart – clothes from Good Will.
- You've got big feet – ears – teeth – nose.
- You look like a pig – baboon – beaver – moron.
- Your barber really scalped you.
- What happened to your hair?
- Did you sleep in that shirt?
- You can't even walk without falling down?
- How could you have missed that ball, it was right over the plate?

Remind the students that they should not continue using this or any other strategy if the bully is becoming violent. Encourage the students to ask an adult if they need help. When asking for help, it is good to tell the adult what strategies you have tried. Ex – "I have ignored Joe's comments, I tried to stay away from him, I responded to him in a neutral way and I asked him to stop. Joe continues to bother me. Can you help me?" Point out how much better this statement would be received by an adult than "Make Joe leave me alone!"

Follow-up
Ask the students:
- Have you ever tried asking the bully to stop bothering you? How did it work?
- Did you learn something today that will help you use the strategy more effectively?
- How does asking the bully to stop take power away from the bully?

I'M CONFUSED
Activity 6.21

Purpose
To teach students to respond to bullies by trying to confuse them.

Materials
Chalkboard, chart or overhead

Procedure
Explain to the students that another way to deal with bullies is to make comments that are confusing to the bully by turning the bullies insult into a compliment. The bully wants to insult and harass you. If you refuse to accept the insult and in fact consider it a complement, it confuses the bully. When you turn the insult or actions into a complement, you may say things like:

- "Why, thank you. What a kind thing to say."
- "That is so sweet of you to want to help me in this way?"
- "Coming from you, that is a real complement."
- "You must really like me because you are having a hard time keeping your hands off me." Alternative ending "Wouldn't spend so much time talking to me."
- "What a sweet thing to say. I didn't know you cared."

(You may want to write these statements so students can refer to them. Encourage the students to add other statements. If you feel any of these comments are too sarcastic, do not use them.)

Role-play with the students by making the following statements and have the students respond by turning the insult into a complement. Tell the student that for this technique to work you need to use an up-beat, positive tone of voice. You can go through the group making a statement to each student and having him/her respond or allow students to raise their hand if they want to respond. After the students have practiced making one response, continue practicing the skill by having them make multiple responses. Skip any statements that would be unsuitable or too sensitive for your students or add statements that may be more appropriate.

- You're short – tall – skinny – fat – clumsy – stupid.
- You're a geek – nerd – egghead – retard – klutz – crybaby – slut.
- You wear glasses – braces – shoes from Wal-Mart – clothes from Good Will.
- You've got big feet – ears – teeth – nose.
- You look like a pig – baboon – beaver – moron.
- Your barber really scalped you.
- What happened to your hair?
- Did you sleep in that shirt?
- You can't even walk without falling down?
- How could you have missed that ball, it was right over the plate?

Tell the students that they should not continue using this or any other strategy if the bully is becoming violent. Remind students that they can always ask an adult for help.

Follow-up
Ask the students:
- Have you ever used this technique with bullies? How did it work?
- What do you like best about this technique?
- How does this technique take power away from the bully?

USE HUMOR
Activity 6.22

Purpose
To help students use humor to defuse the bullies comments.

Materials
Chalkboard, chart or overhead

Procedure
Explain to the students that there are times when humor is an effective way to defuse the power of the bully. Bullies want to control your emotions and make you feel bad. When you respond to their insult with humor, they are not getting the results they want and may stop their bullying. When using this technique, you need to use a very light-hearted tone of voice. When you use humor, you might say something like:

- "Excellent insult! May I use that one?"
- "Can I quote you on that?"
- "Really, and I have wasted all this time thinking I was cute (tall, short, skinny, etc.)"
- "Did you think of that all by yourself?"
- "Wow, how long did it take you to think of that?"
- "What do I look like now?" And make a funny face.
- Just laugh and say "Good one."

(You may want to write some of these statements where students can refer to them. Encourage students to add additional statements. If you feel any of these comments are too sarcastic, do not use them)

Role-play with the students by making the following statements and have the students respond by using humor. Remind the students to use a very light-hearted tone of voice. You can go through the group making a statement to each student and having him/her respond or allow students to raise their hand if they want to respond. After the students have practiced making one response, continue practicing the skill by having them make multiple responses. Skip any statements that would be unsuitable or too sensitive for your students or add statements that may be more appropriate.

- You're short – tall – skinny – fat – clumsy – stupid.
- You're a geek – nerd – egghead – retard – klutz – crybaby – slut.
- You wear glasses – braces – shoes from Wal-Mart – clothes from Goodwill.
- You've got big feet – ears – teeth – nose.
- You look like a pig – baboon – beaver – moron.

Tell the students that they should not continue using this or any other strategy if the bully is becoming violent. Remind students that they can always ask an adult for help.

Follow-up
Ask the students:
- Have you ever used humor to respond to bullies? How did it work?
- When is the best time to use humor with a bully?
- How does humor take power away from the bully?

ASK QUESTIONS
Activity 6.23

Purpose
To teach students to use questions to take power from the bully.

Material
Chalkboard, chart or overhead

Procedures
Teach the students that another way to take power from the bully is to ask questions? When you ask the questions and the bully is put in the position of answering them, you have taken control of the communication. For this technique to be effective you must use an inquisitive tone of voice and must continue asking questions until the bully withdraws from the conversation. If you use this technique, you would say things like:

- "Do you really think so? Who else do you think is weird (skinny, tall, etc.)?"
- "How tall do you think I am? How tall do you have to be to be considered tall? How tall are you?"
- "When did you learn that? What are some other things you know?"
- "Why are you so interested in where I buy my clothes? Where do you buy your clothes? Where did you buy those shoes?"
- "Why are you being so mean to me? Do you think it is cool to be mean? How cool do you think you are?"
- "Why would you want to tell me I am tall (short, clumsy, etc.)? Do you think I don't know I am?
- Do you think that hurts my feelings? Is there a reason you want to hurt my feelings?"
- "Why did you say that? Do you think that is funny? How does saying that make you feel? How do you think it makes me feel?"
- The all time favorite "playing deaf."
- "What did you say? I'm sorry I still didn't hear you. Could you say that again?"

You may want to put some of these responses where students can refer to them.
Encourage students to think of other responses.

Role-play with the students by making the following statements and have the students respond by asking questions. Remind the students to use an inquisitive tone of voice. You can go through the group making a statement to each student and have him/her respond or allow students to raise their hand if they want to respond. After the students have practiced making one response, continue practicing the skill by having them make multiple responses. Skip any statements that would be unsuitable or too sensitive for your students or add statements that may be more appropriate.

- You're short – tall – skinny – fat – clumsy – stupid.
- You're a geek – nerd – egghead – retard – klutz – crybaby – slut.
- You wear glasses – braces – shoes from Wal-Mart – clothes from Good Will.
- You've got big feet – ears – teeth – nose.
- You look like a pig – baboon – beaver – moron.

Tell the students that they should not continue using this or any other strategy if the bully is becoming violent. Remind students that they can always ask an adult for help.

Follow-up
Ask the students:
- Have you ever used questions as a way to respond to bullies? How did it work?
- What would be a good situation in which to use questions with a bully?
- How does asking questions take power away from the bully?

DID THAT MAKE SENSE?
Activity 6.24

Purpose
To help students make responses that can confuse the bully.

Materials
Student handout – **Did That Make Sense?**

Procedure
Instruct the students that another strategy to use with bullies is to say something totally unrelated to the bully's comment that is confusing. With this strategy, you respond to the bully's insult by using some of the same words he used, but you will turn his words into a nonsense statement. Make sure your comments are not rude or insulting. When you take the bully's own words and turn them into a confusing comment, you are taking control of the interaction.

- Give each student the handout and go over the example and make sure the students understand the strategy.
- Review the directions.
- You or a student should read each "bully statement" out loud with emotion.
- Have the students select their answer. (One of the choices is a wrong response and will make the situation worse, one demonstrates another technique that has been taught in other lessons and one response reflects the skill taught in this activity.)
- Move to the next statement and continue through the handout.
- After the students have practiced making one response, continue practicing the skill by having them make multiple responses.

Tell the students that they should not continue using this or any other strategy if the bully is becoming violent. Remind students that they can always ask an adult for help.

Follow-up
Ask the students:
- How is this strategy different from just using humor?
- When do you think this strategy would work best?
- How does turning the bullies comment into a nonsense reply, take away the bully's power?

DID THAT MAKE SENSE?

As each statement is read, select the response that restates the bullies comment in a nonsensical way.

Example:

The bully Says: "<u>Oh, go</u> drop dead."
You say: "<u>Oh, go</u> eat ice cream."

The bully says: "I heard you are dumb as dirt."
  You say:
    1. "Well I heard you have two feet."
    2. "You need to shut up."
    3. "Why did you say that?"

The bully says: "I can't stand being around you."
  You say:
    1. "Then you had better leave or I will throw you out."
    2. "I am sorry you feel that way."
    3. "Yes but can you stand on your hands?"

The bully says: "I am not going to be your friend."
  You say:
    1. "Who wants to be your friend anyway?"
    2. "Well, I'm not going to be your egg plant."
    3. "So!"

The bully says: "I wouldn't come to school if I looked like you."
  You say:
    1. "Well, I wouldn't come to school on Saturday."
    2. "Whatever."
    3. "You really think anyone is uglier than you are?"

I'M CONCERNED ABOUT YOU
Activity 6.25

Purpose
To help students learn to respond to the feeling behind a bullies insults.

Materials
Student handout – *I'm Concerned About You*

Procedure
To the teacher:
This technique is not easy to use and most students will find it too difficult. Review the activity and evaluate the ability level of your group. This may be a good technique to use with peer helpers, peer mediators and other students who exhibit good empathy skills.

Instruct the students that another way to respond to a bully is to identify the negative feeling behind his/her comment or actions. When bullies insult and act aggressively, it is often a response to difficulties and abuse in their own lives. When you respond to the pain behind their hurtful words and actions it can help the bully realize why they are being mean and they may change their behavior. If you respond to the bully's feelings, it shows your concern for their feelings and it may make it more difficult for them to continue being abusive to you.

- Give each student the handout and review the directions.

- You or a student should read each "bully statement" out loud with emotion.

- Have the students select their answer. (One of the choices is a wrong response and will make the situation worse, one demonstrates another technique that has been taught in previous lessons and one response reflects feelings and concern. I found it best to review the responses after each statement to make sure the students are selecting the desired response.

- Move to the next statement and continue through the handout.

- After the students have practiced making one response, continue practicing the skill by having them make multiple responses.

Tell the students that they should not continue using this or any other strategy if the bully is becoming violent. Remind students that they can always ask an adult for help.

Follow-up
Ask the students:
- Have you ever tried responding to the feelings of the bully? How did it work?
- When do you think this strategy would work best?
- How does showing concern for the bully take away the bully's power?

I'M CONCERNED ABOUT YOU

As each statement is read, select the response that best identifies the bully's feelings and shows concern about him/her.

The bully says: "I can't stand being around you!"
You say:
1. "Well you are free to leave if being around me is so difficult."
2. "You must be really angry with me. I don't know what I have done to hurt your feelings."
3. "Well, sit down!"

The bully says: "Get out of my way or I will punch your lights out!"
You say:
1. "Like you could."
2. "You must be really upset to say something like that. Has something happened to you?"
3. "Don't be silly, my lights aren't even on."

The bully says: "You only won because your team cheated."
You say:
1. "I don't blame you for being upset, your team played really well. It is difficult to lose when you played so hard."
2. "You sure are a sore loser."
3. "We didn't cheat and you know it."

The bully says: "I wouldn't be on your crummy team if you begged me."
You say:
1. "Bite me."
2. "I guess we need a broom to sweep up all the crumbs."
3. "I'm sorry that you did not make the team too. I know how it feels to not make the team."

You accidentally bump into the bully and the bully says:
"Hey, watch what you are doing, loser."
You say:
1. "I'm sorry. I know it is upsetting when someone bumps into you."
2. "You could pay more attention too, you know."
3. "Did I lose something, thank you for being so helpful."

The bully says: "You look like a beaver with those teeth."
You say:
1. "You really think I look like a beaver? Don't you think I look more like a rabbit?"
2. "I guess you think making insults is a way to fit in but it really turns people off."
3. "Well that is better than looking like a #$%@ idiot."

The bully says: "You're a #$%& and your mama's one too."
You say:
1. "I didn't know you cared."
2. "Well your mama's a *&%$!"
3. "Something terrible must have happened to make you act so mean."

COMPLIMENT THE BULLY
Activity 6.26

Purpose
To teach students to use compliments to defuse a bully.

Materials
Student handout – **Compliment the Bully**

Procedure
To the teacher:
This technique is not easy to use and most students will find it too difficult. Review the activity and evaluate the ability level of your group. This may be a good technique to use with peer helpers, peer mediators and other students who exhibit good empathy skills.

Instruct the students that another way to respond to a bully's insults is to return the insult with a compliment. This can go against everything we feel, but it is difficult to continue to insult someone when they are giving you compliments. Bullies are often angry and angry people love company. They want you to join them in their anger and their insults are their way of making you angry.

- Give each student the handout and review the directions.

- You or a student should read each "bully statement" out loud with emotion.

- Have the students select their answer. (One of the choices is a wrong response and will make the situation worse, one demonstrates another technique that has been taught in previous lessons and one gives the bully a compliment. I found it best to review the responses after each statement to make sure the students are selecting the desired response.

- Move to the next statement and continue through the handout.

- After the students have practiced making one response, continue practicing the skill by having them make multiple responses.

Tell the students that they should not continue using this or any other strategy if the bully is becoming violent. Remind students that they can always ask an adult for help.

Follow-up
Ask the students:
- Have you ever tried complimenting a bully? How did it work?
- When do you think this strategy would work best?
- How does complimenting the bully take way the bully's power?

COMPLIMENT THE BULLY

As each statement is read, select the response that gives the bully a compliment.

The bully says: "You are a real loser."
You say:
1. "Coming from you that is a real compliment."
2. "I'm sorry you feel that way because I think you are a really nice person."
3. "Well you are a $#%&* head!"

The bully says: "What's with your hair, stick your finger in the light socket or what!"
You say:
1. "I guess my hair is a mess today but may I say your hair looks very nice."
2. "Yea, you should have seen the sparks."
3. "Mind your own business."

The bully says: "That is the ugliest shirt I have ever seen."
You say:
1. "Why, thank you."
2. "This shirt is not as ugly as your mother."
3. "I guess you don't like my clothes but I really like the shirt you are wearing."

The bully says: "I would stay home if I was as ugly as you are."
You say:
1. "I don't like you saying that and I want you to stop."
2. "Eat dirt."
3. "You say mean things but down deep I think you have a good heart."

Unit Seven
Helping the Victim with Special Needs –
Skills for Students With Disabilities

HELPING THE VICTIM WITH SPECIAL NEEDS:

SKILLS FOR STUDENTS WITH DISABILITIES

KIDS WHO ARE DIFFERENT

Here's to the kids who are different,
The kids who don't always get A's,
The kids who have ears twice the size of their peers,
And noses that go on for days...
Here's to the kids who are different,
The kids they call crazy or dumb,
The kids who don't fit, with the guts and the grit,
Who dance to a different drum...
Here's to the kids who are different,
Kids with that mischievous streak,
When they have grown, as history has shown,
It's their difference that makes them unique.

– Digby Wolfe
All Rights Reserved UNM-2004

HELPING THE VICTIM WITH SPECIAL NEEDS

Students with disabilities and those in special education classes are often at greater risk of being bullied because of their lack of academic and social power and because they are often seen as being different by their peers. These students can become the ultimate outsiders and an easy target for bullies.

Students with disorders such as "ADHD" are often referred to as "provocative" victims. The very nature of their disability can result in a lack of impulse control and manifest a myriad of other annoying behaviors. These students often don't stop their behavior without strong correction. I have even heard teachers say, "If I let the students pick on him, maybe he will learn to stop acting that way." If I thought this would work, I might not be so critical but it doesn't work and it is cruel. A "provocative victim" is seen as "asking for it" and "bringing it on him" and is often the person who gets into trouble. A second-grade teacher in Dallas, Texas, was placed on leave after she lined her students up and **ordered** them to hit one of their peers, a student who takes medication daily for emotional problems (Lubbock Avalanche-Journal, May 04.) I contend that teachers have a higher level of responsibility, and must protect students with disabilities from bullying.

If students have the behaviorally disturbed "BD" label and have serious chronic discipline problems, they may be bullies in early education because of grade retention, but they become "provocative victims" in the middle school and high school climate. Some students with disabilities exhibit shyness and difficulty with the social atmosphere and are typically "passive victims." As a result of this, they are at a higher risk.

Students with disabilities must be protected from bullies and be taught the skills they lack. These students must be brought into the mainstream of the student body and made to feel they belong. It is important to help other students understand disabilities and perhaps even provide specific education on certain disabilities. Teachers need to provide opportunities for all students to get to know each other but especially students with disabilities. In our rush to improve test scores we sometimes forget the importance of teaching all students tolerance, kindness and empathy.

STRATEGIES TO HELP STUDENTS WITH SPECIAL NEEDS

1. Present the students with education on bullying and its consequences. (Activities 2.1 *What Is Bullying?*, 2.2 *What Are You Teaching?*, 4.1 *Let's Discuss Bullying*, 4.2 *Bullying Is About Power*, 4.3 *Write About Bullying*, 4.4 *Read About Bullying* & 6.1 *Bullying Inventory*.)

2. Help the student feel a part of the class and assist in increasing communication and bonding within the classroom. This is especially important for students with disabilities. (Activities 2.4 *Breaking Down Fears*, 2.5 *Meet My New Best Friend*, 2.6 *Just Like Me* & 2.7 *Appreciation Time*.)

3. Provide assertiveness training. Many students with disabilities look like victims. These students need to learn to maintain eye contact and stand speak and walk assertively.
   - Make students aware of policies concerning reporting bullying behaviors and instruct them on how to report bullying incidents. (Unit one – *Reporting Bullying Behavior*.)
   - Teach students to look assertive. (Activity 6.2 *Being Assertive Helps*)
   - Teach students to speak assertively. (Activity 6.3 *The "I Messages" Have It*)
   - Instruct students on safety skills. (Activities 6.4 *Think Safety First* & 6.5 *Be Safe Going To and From School*)
   - Recommend to parents that their child participate in private self-defense classes.

4. Help victims deal more effectively with their negative feelings. Students with special needs often harbor feelings of anger, frustration, humiliation and rage. If these students are not able to effectively deal with their feelings they can erupt into violent behaviors, drop out of school and/or carry these negative feelings into their adult lives and relationships.
   - Help students identify and change behaviors and thoughts that are having a negative impact on their self-esteem. (Activity 6.6 *Change Self-Defeating Behaviors*)
   - Present instruction on dealing with negative feelings. (Activities 6.7 *Sticks and Stones*, 6.8 *My Feelings Are Important* & 6.9 *It's Not Fair*)
   - Train students in relaxation techniques and positive visualizations. (Activities 5.2 *Learn to Relax*, 6.10 *Relax* & 6.11 *Relax and Move*)

5. Provide opportunities for **social skills training**. Often victims with special needs who have been mistreated many times are withdrawn and afraid of social interactions. Students who are shy and reserved may have limited social skills. These students often profit from social interactions and skill building with other students, in settings where they may be less afraid to open up and show some leadership.
   - Provide instruction on mediation. (Activity 4.16 *Mediation Works*)
   - Offer opportunities to learn problem solving skills. (Activity 4.15 *Conflicts Have Two Sides*)
   - Conduct classes on friendship. (Activities 4.13 *Lets Be Friends*, 6.12 *Enemies or Friends*, 6.13 *Making Friends*, 6.14 *Treating Others With Respect*.)
   - Provide instruction on response skills and opportunities for practice. (Activities 6.15 *Ignore*, 6.16 *Agree or Disagree*, 6.17 *I'm Not Purple*, 6.18 *I'm Neutral*, 6.19 *Don't Push Back*, 6.20 *Ask Them to Stop*, 6.21 *I'm Confused*, 6.22 *Use Humor*, 6.23 *Ask Questions*, 6.24 *Did That Make Sense?*, 6.25 *I'm Concerned About You*, 6.26 *Complement the Bully*.)
   - Provide opportunities for individual and group counseling. Group interaction is a great place for students with special needs to practice new social skills and build a support group.

STRATEGIES TO HELP STUDENTS WITH SPECIAL NEEDS *(continued)*

6. Help the students **build on their strengths and identify weaknesses.** All students have gifts and talents. Sometimes these talents are not as widely valued by their peers as athletic abilities but they may be highly valued in the adult world. Encourage parents to help by providing private instruction to build their child's skills.

    *   Most students with special needs have areas of giftedness. Teachers should make every effort to identify these areas of giftedness and provide opportunities for students to use their assets in a positive setting.
    *   The school needs to offer a variety of extra-curricular activities for a variety of gifts and talents. When students with special needs participate in extra-curricular activities they experience more of a sense of belonging and friendships among the students.
    *   Teachers and the administration need to recognize and value all talents. The students are more likely to value diverse talents if the staff does.
    *   Provide leadership opportunities for students where they can demonstrate their strengths. Students can tutor, serve as teaching assistants and provide services to the teachers and staff. There are many ways that artistic, musical, writing, academic and organizational skills can be an asset to the school at large.
    *   Students with special interests can share their knowledge with other students in their classes and the school as a whole. The teacher should make an effort to utilize this special interest into the curriculum of their class.
    *   Encourage positive relationships with adults. Students with special needs, especially need an adult within the school whom they can go to for help and support. This relationship needs to be more a mentoring relationship rather that a "teacher's pet." Students who are bullied frequently need an adult who can offer protection, emotional support and assist with problem solving.

7. Improve the student body's understanding of disabilities and provide instruction on how to assist students with special needs.

    *   The teacher needs to create a classroom that appreciates and accepts diversity. (Activity 4.17 *Strength from Diversity*.)
    *   If the student exhibits obvious differences in the abilities and/or behaviors, you may want to educate all students on the nature of the disability and how they can help. This should always be done with the **permission** of the student. (Use the appropriate information found in this unit.)

TEACHER STRATEGIES FOR STUDENTS WITH SPECIAL NEEDS

Regular education teachers are often given the responsibility of dealing with many students with disabilities with little or no training. They must provide special accommodations and make it appear that all students are treated the same. Many teachers begin to resent the additional demands that students with special needs create and can even resent the students. When students have social deficits as well as academic, the job becomes even more overwhelming. Everyone must remember that it is not the student's fault that they have a disability. Their behavior and ability to concentrate will change from day to day and even hour to hour. As frustrating as it is for the teacher, we must realize that it is more frustrating for the student.

Teachers of students with special needs need to:

- Not take the students behavior personally;

- Request that you be given adequate information on the nature of the student's disorder;

- Set high expectations that all students are valued and everyone will be treated with respect;

- Do your best to down play the negative aspects of the student's challenges;

- Provide opportunities for the student with special needs to exhibit his/her strengths without showing obvious favoritism;

- Avoid making the student the "teacher's pet;"

- Identify nonverbal cues to use with the student to indicate that the student needs assistance;

- Identify nonverbal cues to use when the student is off task or needs to become more conscious of his/her behavior;

- Realize that there are some days that will be a wash. Always allow the student to start fresh every day.

ATTENTION DEFICIT HYPERACTIVITY DISORDER

ADHD is a neurobehavioral condition affecting 7 to 12% of children. These students have difficulty regulating their behaviors and they can become under-focused or over-focused. They have a developmentally delayed ability to sustain attention, focus on a task or delay impulsive behavior. Hyperactivity is a factor in some cases and seems to occur more frequently in boys. The symptoms must be observed in more than one setting, have lasted at least six months, and have onset before the age of seven. Students with ADHD can pay attention better to tasks that excites or interest them.

Many of the behaviors associated with ADHD make children targets for bullying because:

1. Students with hyperactivity are often "provocative victims" and can make some feel they deserve the bully's response.

2. Students with ADHD are often restless and often tease and irritate others. They don't pick up cues to know when to stop the annoying behaviors.

3. Impulsive behavior associated with ADHD, cause students to respond before thinking of an appropriate response.

4. The student often has difficulty waiting his/her turn and will interrupt others.

5. They often have short tempers and mood swings.

6. ADHD students have a developmental delay in their executive functioning skills and cannot plan and sequence their behavior as well as others their age.

7. These students can be easily aroused and often become overly emotional.

8. ADHD students may fight back against the bully but are usually ineffective and ends up losing and becomes more embarrassed and frustrated.

9. These students can have difficulty "changing gears" mentally and may try to continue the conflict causing them serious frustration and distress.

CHARACTERISTICS OF ADHD

There are two types of students with ADHD — those who are mainly hyperactive or impulsive (ADHD Predominately Hyperactive) and those who are predominantly inattentive (ADHD Inattentive). Some will embody a mixture of both types (ADHD Combined). If a student has prominent symptoms but does not meet the criteria for the above diagnosis, he/she can be diagnosed with ADHD NOS (ADHD Not Otherwise Specified)

Students with ADHD Predominately Hyperactive:

- Fidgets with hands and /or feet and squirms in seat;

- Often leaves their seat in the classroom when they should not;

- Runs and climbs excessively in places where it is inappropriate;

- Has difficulty playing quietly;

- Are often "on the go" as if "driven by a motor;"

- Usually talks excessively;

- Will blurt out answers before questions have been completed;

- Frequently have difficulty awaiting their turn;

- Regularly interrupts others.

Students with ADHD Predominately Inattentive:

- Often fail to give close attention to details and make careless mistakes;

- Have difficulty holding their attention on a task;

- Frequently do not listen even when being spoken to directly;

- Have difficulty following through with a task and fails to finish schoolwork or chores;

- Have difficulty organizing a task or activity;

- Avoids beginning a task that requires sustained mental attention;

- Often loses things necessary for a task;

- Are easily distracted;

- Are often forgetful of tasks.

DSM-IV, 1994 American Psychological Association

SENSORY INTEGRATION DYSFUNCTION

Sensory integration is the process of organizing the information we get from our bodies and from the world around us for use in daily life. **Sensory Integration Dysfunction (SID)** is the ineffective processing of information received through the senses, causing problems with learning, development, and behavior. No one knows for sure what causes SID. It is estimated that 5 to 20% of children have SID problems significant enough to warrant intervention. Most are boys. Because students with SID have difficulty learning from the feedback in their environment, they often must be taught social skills directly.

SID is an occupational therapy (OT) diagnosis. It can contribute to or exacerbate other problems such as ADHD, pervasive developmental disorders and learning disabilities. The SID student will adamantly avoid or seek out certain sensory stimulations. They may look fine and have superior intelligence but may be awkward and clumsy, fearful and withdrawn, or hostile and aggressive.

Many of the behaviors associated with SID make these children targets for bullying because they:

- Have difficulty with rhythm and have a high or low activity level;

- Demonstrate problems with time management and are chronically late and totally lose track of time;

- Lack awareness of interpersonal distance and what constitutes appropriate and inappropriate touching;

- Misinterpret or fail to understand the meaning of gestures and postures, and lack the inability to use gestures appropriately;

- Lack the ability to accurately "read" facial expressions, maintain eye contact, and use facial expressions with the appropriate intensity;

- Misunderstand or lack the ability to interpret tone of voice, voice volume, etc. They will whistle, hum or clear their throats at inappropriate times;

- Show a failure to understanding the appropriate style of dress and how clothes are worn. Some fail to understand the importance of good personal hygiene.

CHARACTERISTICS OF S.I.D.

If the student adamantly avoids or seeks these behaviors with high frequency and intensity for a long period of time, a professional may need to be consulted for a possible diagnosis. No child will exhibit all the symptoms.

A child with SID:

- Is sensitive to touch and will refuse to touch certain items;

- Is hyper-sensitive to certain clothing and has problems with fabrics, clothing tags and sock seams;

- Enjoys fast-moving or spinning activities;

- Shows caution in approaching fast moving activities;

- Is unusually sensitive to smell;

- Is sensitive to noise or seems to have hearing problems;

- Has a difficulty with speech and/or language skills;

- Seems to have vision problems and can't seem to determine the properties of objects. They cannot tell a hammer is heavy or a knife is sharp;

- Has a "loose" or "floppy" body build and their clothes always seem to hang oddly;

- Has difficulty dressing. They are clumsy putting their arms in the sleeves, putting fingers in mittens, putting on socks, etc.;

- Does not have a definite hand preference when using a spoon, crayon, marker, pencil etc.;

- Avoids games that involve running, jumping, and use of large play equipment;

- Avoids activities involving the manipulation of small objects or the use of crayons, pencils, and scissors;

- Has a short attention span, even with things that they enjoy;

- Tends to be restless or "fidgety" during times when quiet concentration is required;

- Has difficulty regulating his/her sleep patterns.

ASPERGER'S SYNDROME

Asperger's is manifested in impairment in social skills, limited ability to have reciprocal conversations and an intense interest in a special subject. It is usually identified as a Pervasive Developmental Disorder and is considered a subgroup within the autistic spectrum. Asperger's is thought to affect 2 to 4 percent of students and occurs predominantly in boys. Asperger's presents symptoms similar to high-functioning autism. Seldom do students display all the features and some will exhibit only a few of the symptoms.

Many of the characteristic associated with Asperger's make these children targets for bullying. Students with Asperger's syndrome:

- Are delayed or do not develop social interaction skills and are awkward socially with their peers;

- Look like victims because they are often physically clumsy and have difficulty with eye contact;

- Have difficulty understanding the emotions of others and rarely respond appropriately to others;

- Are often horribly misunderstood and are teased or bullied or ignored by others;

- Are hurt by the teasing and often are unaware that their unusual behavior is contributing to the problem;

- Have a limited ability to form friendships and may feel lonely and socially isolated. Other students with Asperger's are perfectly content with no friends;

- Are often isolated which can lead to low self-esteem and this leads to increased isolation and even depression;

- Lack the understanding of non-verbal communication so they continually misunderstand social situations and persist responding inappropriately;

- Rigidly follow social codes of conduct when they are explained. They will be brutally honest once they learn they are expected to be honest;

- Lack the ability to have a shared enjoyment with other people.

CHARACTERISTICS OF ASPERGER'S

If the student has many of these characteristics, a professional may need to be consulted for diagnosis.

Students with Asperger's:

- Don't seem to understand the unwritten rules of social play and repeatedly break the rules without realizing it;

- May avoid social contacts with other children and seems content alone;

- Appears unaware of codes of conduct and makes inappropriate actions and comments;

- Appear to have a lack of empathy for others but really has great difficulty understanding feelings in general;

- Expects you to know their thoughts and experiences even if you were not with them at the time;

- Get upset if things are changed or go wrong;

- Shows emotions out of proportion to the situation. They will laugh loudly when a little giggle is more appropriate;

- Does not like to participate in competitive sports or games. They cannot understand why they should care if their team wins;

- Interprets comments literally. Expressions like "You are a chip off the old block," are very confusing to them;

- Use an unusual tone of voice, monotone or have a formal over-precise speech patterns that can sound like English is not their native language;

- Have difficulty with casual conversation and are more comfortable with the exchange of facts especially concerning their special topic. They seem uninterested in your side of the conversation;

- Have difficulty making little eye contact;

- Reads books for information and are less interested in reading stories;

- Have a preoccupation with one or more special interest that verge on obsession and seems odd to others;

- Have a need for nonfunctional routines or rituals and becomes upset by changes in their schedule;

- Develops elaborate routines that must be completed;

- Has poor motor coordination and clumsiness;

- Has an unusual fear or areas of distress;

- May rock when excited or distressed.

AUTISTIC DISORDER
Pervasive Developmental Disorder

Autism is characterized by a severe delay or abnormal functioning in social interactions, language and/or social communication, and imaginative play. Autism has a wide variety of functioning from severe (nonverbal, totally aloof, and highly repetitive) to high-functioning students who are only mildly socially awkward and have special interests very similar to student with Asperger's.

Autistic behaviors must be observed before age three. The disorder is thought to affect up to 6 % of the population and two-thirds to three-quarters of those students are high-functioning.

Social interactions must include at least two of the following characteristics:

- A developmental inappropriate use of multiple nonverbal communication skills such as eye contact, facial expression, body postures, and gestures in social interactions;

- A marked failure to develop peer relationships appropriate to developmental level;

- A lack of desire to share enjoyment, interests, or achievements with other people. The child would not show, bring or point out objects of interest;

- A marked lack of the ability to carry on social and/or emotional reciprocity in interpersonal interactions.

Impairments in communication must be demonstrated in at least one of the following areas:

- A marked delay in or total lack of, the development of the spoken language. The child does not compensate for lack of verbal communication with gestures or miming;

- The child has adequate speech but fails to initiate or sustain a conversation with others;

- A lack of varied, spontaneous make-believe play or social imitative play appropriate to their developmental level;

- A marked preoccupation with one or more stereotyped and restricted pattern of interest that is abnormal in intensity.

DSM IV 1994 American Psychological Association

MENTAL RETARDATION

Students are considered mentally retarded when they have an IQ of 70 or below on an individually administered IQ test with impairments in adaptive functioning (self-care, home living, social/interpersonal skills, use of community resources, self-direction, functional academic skills, work, leisure, health, and safety.)

- Mild Mental Retardation: IQ level 50-55 to 70
- Moderate Mental Retardation: IQ level 35-40 to 50-55
- Severe Mental Retardation: IQ level 20-25 to 35-40
- Profound Mental Retardation: IQ level below 20 or 25

LEARNING DISORDERS

Students are considered to have a learning disorder when academic achievement is substantially below that expected, based on the person's chronological age and measured intelligence.

Reading Disorder -
Reading achievement is substantially below that expected, based on intelligence.

Mathematics Disorder -
Mathematical ability is substantially below that expected, based on intelligence.

Disorder of Written Expression -
Writing skills are substantially below those expected, based on intelligence.

MOTOR SKILLS DISORDER

Developmental Coordination Disorder –
Students are considered to have a coordination disorder when coordination in daily activities is substantially below that expected of a person based on age and intelligence. This may include delays in developmental milestones (e.g., walking, crawling, and sitting) clumsiness, poor handwriting, and poor performance in sports.

COMMUNICATION DISORDERS

Expressive Language Disorder –

Students are considered to have an expressive language disorder when there is a substantial deficit in the ability to express themselves verbally, based on age and intelligence. The disturbance may be manifested by symptoms that include limited vocabulary, making errors in tense, or having difficulty recalling words or producing sentences.

Mixed Receptive-Expressive Language Disorder –

Students are considered to have a mixed language disorder when receptive and expressive language development is substantially below that expected, based on age and intelligence. Symptoms may include those of Expressive Language Disorder as well as difficulty understanding words, sentences, or specific types of words, such as spatial terms.

Phonological Disorder –

Students are considered to have a phonological disorder when there is a failure to use developmentally expected speech sounds that are appropriate for age and dialect. The child will make errors in sound production, use substitutions of one sound for another or omit a sound.

Stutter –

Students are considered to have a stutter disorder when there is a disturbance in the normal fluency and time patterning of speech. Stuttering is characterized by sound repetitions, broken words, pauses in speech and an excess of physical tension.

WHAT CAN YOU DO TO HELP?

One of the real challenges for anti-bullying programs is helping kids who just don't get it. There are students who seem impervious to the nonverbal messages, who scream at other kids, invade their space, talks too loudly and may smell bad. Many teachers also find them irritating. These students can not read social cues.

The teacher can:

- Help to identify the child's problem areas. In a private conference, let the child know what is going on and the skills they are lacking;

- Form a partnership with the child to work on developing skills in his/her problem area(s);

- Provide instruction on skills the child is lacking or having difficulty with;

- Describe the situation the child wants to participate in and discuss how others feel;

- Help the children "read" situations and identify what they should do or say and shouldn't do or say;

- Provide opportunities for structured skill building activities with the student and the rest of the class.

TEACHING NONVERBAL COMMUNICATION SKILLS

RHYTHM AND USE OF TIME

Help the student learn to recognize the rhythms of others and teach him/her to adjust his/her rhythms to match those of others.

- Vary your speed of hand clapping and ask the child to stay with you as you change from one rate to another.
- Have the child perform speaking, playing, or writing at different speeds.
- Use a timer to guide the child's rate of asking or responding to questions.
- Have the child approximate the passage of various amounts of time. For example – when thirty seconds or one minute has passed.
- Have the child observe the rates of various behaviors in others (e.g. swinging, running, walking) and try to match those rates.
- Describe situations in which it would be appropriate for the child to slow or increase the speed of behavior. Have the student role play these situations.
- Determine the child's best time of day and plan to save the most difficult activities for that time.

Help a child develop better time skills.

- Teach time estimation skills. Give the student an assortment of tasks and/or assignments. Have him/her estimate how long it will take to complete each task.
- Practice estimating accurate travel times. Identify some places that your child must go and provide a target time for his/her arrival. Have the child estimate a travel time and give a starting time in order to arrive on time.
- Discuss the meanings of punctuality: What does being late mean to a friend who is waiting for you? What does it mean to keep your teacher waiting? You grandparents? What are some of the consequences of being late in each of these situations?
- Monitor the number of times the student is late.
- Encourage the parents to provide their child with a watch that has a built-in timer.
- Have the student use a timer and begin to monitor the amount of time it takes to perform certain tasks.
- Have the child keep track of the punctuality and use of time by others, such as parents, teachers, or peers.
- Talk about situations in which people do not control their time efficiently. Discuss the consequences of mismanaging time in each of the situations.

USE OF SPACE AND TOUCH

Help the student become more aware of his/her personal boundaries.

- Have the student observe people sitting together on benches or sofas or standing in line for lunch or to buy tickets. Point out that unless there is a good reason, they are not touching each other.
- Teach the student how to estimate and maintain appropriate personal space.
    - Intimate space - 18 inches
    - Personal space - 4 feet
    - Social space - 12 feet
    - Public space - beyond 12 feet

    Discuss behavior and conversations that are suitable at each distance.
- Have several students seated in movable chairs at a table. Have another student enter the group and help the students see how to adjust their space to accommodate the additional student. Continue to bring students to the table and teach students to adjust.
- Make a six-foot measurement on the floor. Have the student imagine another person at the end. Have him/her move toward the person and stop at the distance he/she feels would be appropriate. Examples might include: parents, teachers, police, principals, friends, strangers, etc.

Help the student learn about appropriate touching.

- Instruct the student regarding the areas of his/her body that may be touched in public.
- Discuss the appropriate touching of others and the suitable intensity of the touching. Some examples of questions for discussion:
    - When you are trying to get someone's attention with a touch, where do you touch them?
    - What should you say?
    - Where is it okay to touch Mom versus a teacher?
    - When is okay to touch Mom at home, Mom in town, etc?
- Discuss what is being communicated through touching. Practice the appropriate intensity of a hug, handshake, pat on the back, a tap on the shoulder. Identify what is being communicated when a person refuses to be touched.
- Role-play situations and have the child practice appropriate touching. Provide the student with feedback concerning their touching.
- Call the students attention to people touching each other in natural settings. Try to identify what the student can learn about peoples' relationships based on their touching. When a teacher is touching another child, is the teacher pleased with the student or upset? Help the student determine if it is appropriate for him/her to touch the others in the same way?
- Discuss how other people feel about being touched. How does a person feel when someone cannot keep his/her hands to him/herself? Why is it a problem to sit so close to a stranger?

GESTURES AND POSTURES

Help the student develop better communication skills through gestures and postures.

- Get parental permission to make a video tape of the student in routine activities. Watch the tape together with the volume turned off. Help the student identify positive and negative postures and gestures they are using. Discuss whether the posture or gesture is appropriate of the situation.
- Watch TV shows or movies with the student. Periodically stop the tape and help the student identify the relationships between the characters. Connect the characters' gestures with their emotional states and discuss how this information can help you know how to respond to people. Help the child predict what may happen next.
- If there is cultural diversity in your school or the student's home, discuss differences in gestures in different cultures.
- Play games such as charades, to allow the student to practice using gestures or other nonverbal means of communication. Have the students play charades with feelings as well as situations.
- Look through books and magazines and identify the meaning of postures and gestures in pictures (tired, bored, angry, excited, happy, etc.)

FACIAL EXPRESSIONS

Help the student learn to communicate and read facial expressions more successfully.

- Discuss the importance of eye contact. What does making eye contact communicate when someone is talking to you? What is being communicated when you refuse to make eye contact?
- Have the student make a dictionary of facial expressions. Allow the student to draw or cut out pictures and label the feeling a person with that expression would have.
- Use facial-expression flash cards. Ask the student to identify the expression on the card or have the child act out an appropriate response to that expression.
- Have the student practice facial expressions in front of mirror. Call out feelings (fear, anger, sadness, and happiness) and have the student make the facial expression.
- Play charades using only facial expressions.
- Describe various situations (you won the game, lost the game, hurt yourself, made a good grade, etc.) and have the student make the appropriate facial expression to respond to that situation.
- Watch a movie without the sound. Have the student focus on the facial expressions of the characters and try to determine what is happening between the characters. Occasionally stop the tape and ask the child to predict what might happen next.
- Encourage the student to observe people's faces and try to detect what their relationship is and the nature of their discussion.

TONE, LOUDNESS AND NOISES

Helping a child learn to understand the meaning of tone of voice, loudness and other noises.

- Have the student listen to a tape and ask him/her to use tone of voice cues to portray the facial expressions, postures, and/or gestures of the person talking.